A GENTLEMAN'S GUIDE
TO MANNERS, SEX, AND RULING THE WORLD

S. K. Baskerville

A GENTLEMAN'S GUIDE
to Manners, Sex, and Ruling the World

How to Survive as a Man in the Age of
Misandry — and Do So with Grace

SOPHIA INSTITUTE PRESS
Manchester, New Hampshire

Sophia Institute Press
Box 5284, Manchester, NH 03108
1-800-888-9344

www.SophiaInstitute.com

Sophia Institute Press® is a registered trademark of Sophia Institute.

paperback ISBN 978-1-64413-463-4
ebook ISBN 978-1-64413-464-1
Library of Congress Control Number: 2021936824

First printing

For John Haskins and Ed Truncellito,
exemplars of the gentlemanly ideal

*Society everywhere is in conspiracy
against the manhood of every one of its members.*

—Emerson

CONTENTS

PREFACE

What authority does one man have to pronounce upon the behavior of other men and tell them the right and wrong way to live their lives? As much as anyone else, I suppose, since no official rules have ever been codified for either manners or manhood, other than the test of time and the willingness of readers to accept what a given writer prescribes. I have tried to overcome this limitation by consulting my predecessors over the ages and competitors today. Advice books for men go back to the Middle Ages and continue to issue forth from the presses and the Internet. Since recent versions depart significantly from the classics and from one another, I have not hesitated to indicate where I disagree and have left the reader to choose. I have not tried to cover every detail of, for example, table manners or sartorial style that might be desirable for the modern gentleman. Existing books treat the more obvious points, and nowadays details are readily available on the Internet. My aim here is to point the reader in the right direction and provide him with the larger principles that will help in distinguishing good advice from bad.

For convenience, the book is divided into fairly detailed subheadings, so that different subjects may be consulted individually. A certain logic is intended in the organization, however, and readers might therefore benefit from reading most of it in the order presented.

⟜

I am grateful to Sophia Institute Press and to Michael Warren Davis for many sensible suggestions and some substantive points.

A GENTLEMAN'S GUIDE
TO MANNERS, SEX, AND RULING THE WORLD

INTRODUCTION

Being a man is not easy nowadays. You never know what is expected of you. Feminists call you sexist if you act like a man, and traditionalists call you a wimp if you do not. You think that—

But hold on just a minute there. Come, man. Pull yourself together! Away with this unseemly self-pity! When was it ever "easy to be a man"? At one time you were expected to fight and likely die to protect your home and homeland against enemies both foreign and domestic, which few men nowadays must do. Your life expectancy in 1900 was forty-seven, and in 1500 it was a fraction of that, whereas today it is around eighty-one. Men have always been required to accept responsibility and sacrifice themselves for others. Let us not forget the lines of Kipling:

> If you can keep your head when all about you
> Are losing theirs and blaming it on you,
>
> If you can bear to hear the truth you've spoken
> Twisted by knaves to make a trap for fools,
>
> Yours is the Earth and everything that's in it,
> And—which is more—you'll be a Man, my son.

And besides, why are you reading a self-help book in the first place? Self-help books are for women.

Do you see the problem? Being a man today may not be more difficult, but it is different than in the past — and in ways that are not easy to understand. Manhood has always been something that must be achieved and proven, and it always will be. But today the most serious threats to your masculinity do not come from the next man's masculinity: the bully on the block or a rival in love. Today your manhood is threatened by a hostile culture and an aggressive political climate that resents masculinity itself, demonizes it as "toxic," and seeks to diminish, "redefine," or even eradicate it altogether. In the past, if a man felt deficient in manhood, the clear remedy was to acquire more: fencing lessons, Charles Atlas courses, workouts in the gym. But paradoxically, becoming more manly today is precisely what many men are afraid to do.

And yet, while we must all mouth the new pieties, it is also clear that most people nowadays want and expect men to act like men. This includes most women.

In the past, a man measured his manhood by his status in the world, which was itself determined in various ways: not only physical strength and courage but wealth, income, professional prestige, and military service. But today more is involved than simply an individual man's status. A man's status is directly connected with larger crises in the relations between men and women, which is being constantly recast in ways that no one fully understands and no one can control. Traditional advice books on manners and gentlemanly behavior always claimed that manhood was defined by certain universal principles, but inevitably they also tailored their advice according to the cultural norms of their day. Now the norms have changed even more fundamentally. This may mean that new advice is needed, but at the least it means that even the standard advice, tried and true as much of it remains, requires new formulations. Some of the rules have fallen into abeyance for so long that they now need to be not simply stated but explained. Today it is not even clear what the norms are from one day to the next. While norms are always changing, the rapid changes of the last few decades bear directly on the question "What is a man?"

What Is a Gentleman?

In civilized society—and especially throughout the English-speaking world[1]—being a man means being a *gentleman*. What precisely is a "gentleman"? This question has been the subject of extended debate for centuries, in novels, plays, films, essays, histories, and advice books like this one. Here we will push the envelope a bit. To be a gentleman is much more than (as some books from past centuries felt it necessary to advise) learning to look at the ceiling when belching, not peering into your hand-kerchief after you blow your nose, or refraining from cooling your coffee by pouring it into the saucer. And one guidebook further insists that it is considered bad form to strike an enemy while he is defecating.[2]

---

[1] No precise equivalent of this word seems to exist in any other language, reflecting its specific development in England and countries influenced by it. Hugo Jacomet explains why he must avoid a literal translation into the French *gentilhomme* for his book *The Parisian Gentleman* in a YouTube video entitled "Être un *gentleman* au 21ème siècle" (my emphasis).

[2] Henry Hitchings, *Sorry! The English and Their Manners* (New York: John Murray, 2013), 21.

A GENTLEMAN'S GUIDE

Being a gentleman is a more serious matter than the colloquial usage of being polite and considerate of others, as when we tell boys to "be a gentleman." Being a gentleman means accepting responsibility, first, for oneself, and then as well for one's family, community, and country. It is essential to being an effective citizen and a leader. Valuing the gentleman may well be the distinguishing feature of our civilization.

Misconceptions abound about what it means to be a gentleman. Perhaps the most unhelpful is that it is a status into which one must be "to the manor born"—that is, with the right parentage, family background, and upbringing. But this is directly contrary to the ideal and to the history as it has been formulated by some of our greatest minds. It is true that, ideally, gentlemanly conduct is something a man learns from his father and passes on to his son. This has never been reliable, however, and it is especially unreliable today. So at least since the Renaissance, older men of the governing class have been writing advice manuals like this one addressed to younger men not only of their own class but also to newcomers and *parvenus*, instructing them on how to behave in accordance with the norms of the class into which they aspire to membership. Peasants moving to the cities and working their way up through the social ranks had to be instructed on how to stop behaving like bumpkins and start acting the part of civilized urban dwellers, citizens, and even rulers. Castiglione's *The Courtier* and Machiavelli's *The Prince* are only the most outstanding examples, if not entirely typical.

One of the recurring themes over the centuries is that merit and practice are far more important than ancestry in establishing a gentleman. Indeed, there was no point in writing the advice books in the first place if gentlemanly status was simply inherited or absorbed from one's aristocratic ancestors, as if by osmosis.

Many renowned gentlemen started life as the humblest common-
ers, and some began worse than that. The advice writers themselves were at pains to emphasize that low origins are nothing
to be ashamed of. "Neither are the truly valorous, or in any way
virtuous, ashamed of their so mean parentage," wrote Sir Henry
Peacham in *The Compleat Gentleman* (1634), "but rather glory
in themselves, that their merit hath advanced them above so
many thousands far better descended."[3] One reason the English
aristocracy managed to survive to the present day—long after
their French counterparts were having their heads removed—was
because the English aristocracy was an "open elite" into which
newcomers were, if not exactly welcomed, at least able to pen-
etrate—but only after they had learned to behave appropriately.
It might require a generation or two for the children of the new
arrivistes to be properly instructed in the correct manners from
an early age before they would be fully accepted as equals. But
that is why the books existed, to equip the sons with the education and social graces to be admitted into circles from which the
fathers had been excluded. As Americans and other colonials
took over the ideal, it became even less tied to elite families
with aristocratic titles and came to be the model as well for the
republican gentleman and democratic citizen.

This, is turn, points to a larger truth that you may find helpful
to know from the start: being a gentleman—being a man—is
never effortless, however much part of the ideal may be to make
it appear that way. It requires conscious and even strenuous effort.
Today, one of the greatest impediments to becoming a man may
be an ironic snobbery that manliness is something to be ridiculed,
which is usually combined with the secret desire for some men

---

[3]   *Peacham's Compleat Gentleman,* 1634 (Oxford: Clarendon, 1906), 5.

to believe that they are above having to make a conscious effort. No man is ashamed of being masculine, after all. But men are often ashamed of aspiring to be more masculine than they presently are and of having to work to improve themselves, as if the aspiration itself and the effort reveal inadequacy. It is this secret fear that the culture today exploits to denigrate manhood.

We cannot all be born into an earldom, and none of us is born with six-inch biceps or a classical education. But some of these things we can achieve, if not at one point in life then at another, and we are only at fault to the extent that we do not try. (The lives of Theodore Roosevelt and Winston Churchill are often held up as examples of heroic men born with great physical disadvantages.)[4]

So get over this idea right now that you cannot be a gentleman, or that it is too late for you, or that you are adopting some kind of false persona, or that it is "just not me." Any man can be a gentleman, and it is never too late. It is the goal to which every man should aspire. Being a gentleman is not a matter of family, or ancestry, or going to the right schools, or having the right accent, or wearing the right clothes, or knowing the right people, or going to the right clubs, sporting competitions, or cultural events. You are not required to attend Henley Regatta, hunt wild boar in the Ardennes, or crook your little finger while (excuse me, *whilst*) drinking tea.[5] Being a gentleman is a state of mind,

---

[4] See Frank Miniter, *The Ultimate Man's Survival Guide: Rediscovering the Lost Art of Manhood* (Washington, DC: Regnery, 2009), locs. 1339 and 3008, Kindle.

[5] As one historian lists the accoutrements: "ancestry, accent, education, deportment, mode of dress, patterns of recreation, type of housing, and style of life." David Cannadine, *Class in Britain* (New Haven: Yale University Press, 1998), 22.

though it is also one that must nevertheless be put into practice in daily life. As Richard Steele wrote over three centuries ago, "The appellation of *Gentleman* is never to be affixed to a man's circumstances, but to his behaviour in them."[6]

So remember the old adage — repeated again and again over the centuries to remind even the most illustrious that they, too, had "their place" — that while a king can create a duke, an earl, a viscount, a marquis, a baron, or a knight, "the king cannot make a gentleman."[7]

Today, the traditional advice manuals and "courtesy" books may seem quaint and out of date. It is not my intention here to instruct you, as does one late-medieval authority, on "when,

---

[6]   Richard Steele, "207: 5th August 1710," in *The Tatler*, vol. 3, ed. Donald F. Bond (Oxford: Oxford University Press, 1987), 99–100, quoted in Christine Berberich, *The Image of the English Gentleman in Twentieth-Century Literature: Englishness and Nostalgia* (Aldershot, Hampshire, UK: Ashgate, 2007), 6n16.

[7]   "A king might ennoble a man by giving him his coat of arms … but he would no more have thought of creating him a gentleman than of creating him a giant." Attributed to John Selden, also to James I: David Castronovo, *The English Gentleman: Images and Ideals in Literature and Society* (New York: Ungar, 1987), 7. The tension — often the discrepancy — between the gentleman as an existing and accepted social status and as a normative ideal pervades the traditional literature and forms a prominent theme in the celebrated novels of the nineteenth century. As these paragraphs indicate, I will assume that the latter definition has largely won the day and treat it as a moral ideal to which any and all may aspire. Still, we might preserve a bit of the older ideal with the possibility that an accomplished gentleman can pass on his status to his sons (for which, see below under "Children"). The only other exception that comes to mind today is some members of the legal profession who feel entitled to place the letters "Esq." following their name.

where, and how you can urinate, defecate, spit, belch, and fart politely," though it might be worth pondering the wisdom behind the stipulation that "only the head of household was entitled to urinate in the hall." And yes, you would probably do well to ensure that the toilets in your home are "situated so as to keep unpleasant smells to a minimum."[8] But while the application of the rules may change with circumstances, the principles underlying them remain essentially the same.

You may also think that some features of a gentleman I describe are stodgy and my strictures old-fashioned. But before you dismiss them, do consider one thing: the decline of the gentlemanly ideal has been followed quickly by the decline of the manly ideal. Once gentlemen lost their unique status, no men could keep theirs for long.

⌒

The required state of mind can begin right now. Being a gentleman means that you must resolve to adopt a code of behavior that will change not only the way you behave but the way you think of yourself, the way you comport yourself, the way you interact with others, and the way others perceive you. You must adopt behavior that will put you above even the suspicion of reproach, and you must make it a habit.

Etiquette books often emphasize that the basic principles of manners can be reduced to showing "respect" to others. But I will add that you must also command respect yourself, and the

---

[8] John Gillingham, "From *Civilitas* to Civility: Codes of Manners in Medieval and Early Modern England," *Transactions of the Royal Historical Society* 12 (2002): 267–289, 274.

giving and receiving often interact together and reinforce each other. "It is almost a definition of a gentleman to say he is one who never inflicts pain," wrote Cardinal John Henry Newman. "He has too much good sense to be affronted at insults.... [He is] too well employed to remember injuries, and too indolent to bear malice."[9]

Yet as Newman's words make clear, being a gentleman does not mean you will never offend and anger people. If you are afraid to offend and anger, then you are not yet fully a man. If you have enemies, Winston Churchill is credited with saying, "that means you've stood up for something, sometime in your life." There are times when a man cannot avoid angering people. At the risk of angering some people myself right now, I will suggest the specifically masculine quality of this principle. The essence of femininity is to inspire love. A man, by contrast, has responsibilities that will place him in positions where he must not be afraid of being hated. But you must never offend and anger people for frivolous or personal reasons. You must reserve this option for only the most important matters. As Oscar Wilde is said to have remarked, "A gentleman never offends unintentionally."[10]

In fact, a large part of being a gentleman is, and always has been, determined by the way you respond to insults, attacks, accusations, slanders, libels, and injuries. Of course, the art of both giving and receiving constructive criticism with tact and diplomacy is also part of the package, but even that is not enough. When, despite your impeccable behavior, you are attacked—and you will be—you must respond with both restraint and courage. This may no longer mean pistols at dawn, but neither does it mean running to teacher—or to lawyers, judges, and policepersons—with every injury you consider "unfair."

Leadership

Mention was made earlier of history's most famous advice books for the social and political elite, *The Courtier*, by Castiglione, and *The Prince* of Machiavelli. But few of us will likely be Italian Renaissance courtiers or adventurer-princes. Much more influential for the average English-speaking gentleman was Thomas Elyot's *Book Named the Governour* (1531), and its many imitators. The title indicates that Elyot was concerned with the gentleman's role in ruling, as we are here, but it would be more accurate to say that he was convinced that just to *be* a gentleman, even quite an ordinary one, inevitably involved an element of ruling.[11] This did not necessarily mean becoming a politician and assuming the reins of government in order to tell everyone else what to do; far from it. In the first instance, it simply meant learning to exercise authority over the limited space that a man had been given in life.[12] This started with the principle of learning to rule

[11] Elyot (like other English writers) says that education is "to fit a gentleman for authority in the commonwealth." William Pocock, *Doctrine of the English Gentleman* (Canada: William Pocock, 2017), loc. 2256, Kindle.

[12] One of today's more sensible books on manhood puts the principle in clear contemporary terms: "Every man has been given territory.... This territory is defined by what a man is responsible for. The key to powerful manhood is that a man fully owns— takes responsibility for, tends, stands guard over, assures the healthy condition of—the field assigned to him. When a man first starts out in the world, he may only be responsible for half a dorm room and a rusty car. He might also have a part-time

himself and extended from there to his family and household, sharing in the affairs of the local community, and onward, if occasion served, to larger duties, unofficial and perhaps eventually official. Of critical importance to the English conception of the gentleman was that the duties of governing one's allotted domain were usually carried out as an *amateur* rather than a professional. A paid professional administrator or civil servant is part of a bureaucracy and must follow the orders of a superior. A gentleman serves others out of a sense of civic duty, using his own discretion and moral judgment—and often at his own expense of time and money. This is more than a platitude or a perfunctory exhortation to selfless altruism because it also means that he carries out his duties how and when—and sometimes even if—his discretion tells him he should.

This ideal was imported to America and was especially decisive in the mid-Atlantic region, where gentry sons became the country's leaders before, during, and long after the American Revolution. This is why Virginia, which was settled by many second sons of the English gentry, became the "mother of presidents."

In other words, a gentleman is foremost a citizen, not a functionary. While he values competence and diligence, he has neither the time nor the requirement to "muddy his hands" by trying to

---

job, schoolwork, and the care of body and soul to think about. These things make up his field. It's what he's responsible for. All of it. If he's a serious man who knows something of genuine manhood, he tends these things with zeal and devotion. They comprise the field assigned to him for his season of his life. And he knows that real men tend their fields." Stephen Mansfield, *Mansfield's Book of Manly Men: An Utterly Invigorating Guide to Being Your Most Masculine Self* (Nashville: Thomas Nelson, 2013), 25.

acquire a thorough professional expertise in all the unpredictable exigencies that may demand his attention—even in the event that he does become some kind of paid official. He must learn how to "muddle through." Remember the succinct lines of those renowned authorities on gentlemanly conduct, Gilbert and Sullivan:

> Of legal knowledge I acquired such a grip
> That they took me into the partnership.
> And that junior partnership, I ween,
> Was the only ship that I ever had seen.
>
> But that kind of ship so suited me,
> That now I am the ruler of the Queen's Navee![13]

⤳

This book, therefore, has two purposes. One is to help you as a man survive and even thrive in an age that is increasingly hostile to men, manhood, and masculinity—and moreover, to do so with grace and elegance. But more, in helping you both define and protect yourself, it will also serve a larger purpose: to help you understand how for you, as a man, it is your task also to ensure that, along with yourself, your family, friends, associates, community, and the larger institutions of our society and civilization survive and thrive.

"Wait just a minute," I hear you say. "I never signed on for this when I bought this book. I just wanted to learn how to be like David Niven or Laurence Olivier, to tie a bowtie, mix a martini,

---

[13] W. S. Gilbert and Arthur Sullivan, "When I Was a Lad," song 9 in *H.M.S. Pinafore* (1878).

and dance a quadrille." Sorry, you were signed up for it at birth. By your very existence as a man, you have taken the king's shilling, and you are engaged. Responsibility comes with the DNA.

Being a man has always meant being a leader, and it always will mean that. All the best books on manhood emphasize this, though often without explaining why.[14] Leadership is not an option but an imperative; it, too, comes with the Y chromosome. Your leadership may involve only small matters at first and most of the time. But even these may be your training for greater eventualities, and you must be prepared.

This, too, is more than the platitude you may think it is and that some have made it. A lot of nonsense is written about leadership, so it is important to understand what it is — and what it is not. Leadership is not about being the first to speak or grab the stage or the microphone or the spotlight. It is not about proclaiming to the world that you alone have the solution to whatever you yourself have determined to be the problem and that everyone should follow you. Quite the opposite. It really begins with humility, and the best leader is often the last to speak. In fact, the greatest leaders in history often did not want the role in the least and tried their best to wiggle out of it. Moses is the classic example of the reluctant leader, offering God a litany of excuses and then, when they ran out, just begging God to choose someone else. God was not pleased.

Leadership is not about trying to have your way or shape the world in your own image. It is not about taking on some grand and glorious cause that you think entitles you to impose your

---

[14] For example, Brett and Kate McKay, *The Art of Manliness: Classic Skills and Manners for the Modern Man* (Cincinnati: How Books, 2009), chap. 7.

preferences or opinions on others in your idealistic aspiration to "change the world" or "make the world a better place." This is the prescription less for a leader than for a troublemaker, and many would-be leaders are precisely that. Your first duty is to protect yourself, your family, and others close to you, and often what you will need to protect them from are the unintended discomforts and dangers that result because of all the other would-be leaders who are endeavoring to change the world and make it a better place. If accepting this duty leads on to greater things, then you could become a great leader, but seldom does it start with that ambition.

Leadership is about stepping into the role when no one else wants it. It is about assuming responsibilities that no one else will take on. True leadership requires sacrifice and courage, not glory — or at least it means postponing the glory for quite a long time, though that, too, may come your way in the end.

To grasp why leadership is inseparable from manhood — and different from grandstanding — you must understand why leadership begins with yourself: in a small way, you must exercise it simply to survive, because ultimately you have no one to rely on but yourself. When women have fears or grievances, they can enlist others to fight their battles for them. At one time, codes of gallantry assigned that task to men like you: to slay the dragons and otherwise allay the fears, provide for the needs, protect, and right the wrongs of women. The basic principle itself has not really changed, for all these duties still remain. But now we are seeing the consequences of not honoring it. For nowadays the task is more likely to fall to paid professional dragon slayers: police, lawyers, judges, and civil servants, whose jobs and salaries depend on finding as many dragons to slay as possible and, if necessary, conjuring them up where they do not really exist. Many of the professional dragon slayers will therefore quite readily see *you* as a dragon and be more than happy to allay the fears of women and right their wrongs by slaying you. In any case, you have only yourself. You therefore can survive as a man and exercise the leadership that will help others survive, and not only can you achieve these two aims simultaneously, but it is the premise of this book that there is no other way for either to be achieved than for them to be achieved together.

After yourself, leadership extends to those closest to you and those for whom you have responsibility: principally your family. When they are injured or aggrieved, it is you who must defend them. If anyone else assumes that task for you—whether it is a neighbor, a lawyer, a judge, a social worker, or some other official—then your family belongs to them, not you. The code of leadership does not require you to defend the entire world and everyone in it from everyone else in it. You need to defend, first and foremost, those you love, for that is the most effective way to show them your love. Words alone have nowhere near the same effect. From there, if it becomes necessary, you will discover if and when your neighborhood, community, region, country, or the rest of humanity also need you.

"Unfortunately, many men today are sloughing off leadership responsibilities either because of laziness or apathy," laments one of today's popular advice books. "They would rather live a life of ignoble ease and have others shoulder the responsibility for them."[15] This is the lamentation of every age, and of course it is always to some extent true. But it is also a cliché and therefore meaningless. For this is not the whole story. If it were, then that author's exhortations to manliness would be adequate, and the present book would not be necessary.

---

[15] McKay, *Art of Manliness*, 208.

It is true that men as a group have made a lot of mistakes in recent decades and have often failed in their leadership responsibilities. But you need to understand what these responsibilities were in the first place in order to understand where the failures occurred and how not to fail yourself in the future. A gentleman always accepts constructive criticism, but he also discerns which criticism is well-intentioned and truly constructive and which is malicious and self-serving. You are not required to accept the scolding of every armchair moralizer who wants to convince you that being more of a man means acting more like a woman.

If our age is different, it is not because men are different but because nowadays they are cowed into withdrawal and submission by an elite culture that is hostile to masculinity itself and threatens to punish men simply for acting like men when they *do* exercise leadership. These threats involve not the standard physical dangers, nor the traditional forms of tyranny. Like the HIV virus that attacks not this or that organ but rather the immune system, which protects everything else, today's challenge to one's masculinity is not an external danger but an attack on masculinity itself.

This diabolical strategy calls for a special response. For while the fundamental principles and rules of manly behavior have not changed, they do need to be reformulated. You are still required to accept all the traditional duties of manhood, including deference to, and sacrifice for, women. But now you must do more.

Some men today have been tempted into various forms of disengagement or withdrawal. Indeed, some have tried to turn disengagement and withdrawal into a virtue. The argument often runs that when we are up against forces that are overwhelmingly powerful, we have no choice but to withdraw from the world.

The most powerful such response has been the movement known as "Men Going Their Own Way" (MGTOW). These men now produce Internet videos by the thousands which are viewed by the millions. The gist of their argument is that men should withdraw and disengage from marriage, family life, women generally, or society altogether for fear that otherwise they could end up being sued, fired, jailed, or just generally having their lives ruined by one form of trumped-up accusation or another, by some woman with a grievance.

Factually, these men have almost everything in their favor. Their assessment of the reality is virtually unassailable, and their complaints cannot be dismissed. Their response is much more than puerility, as the attacks on them invariably have attempted to depict it. Indeed, the attacks against them have usually been far more superficial and devoid of thought than what they themselves exhibit.

But their solution has serious drawbacks and dangers. For if they are making withdrawal a virtue for its own sake, then they are denying an essential part of their manhood, which, again, must be to lead. While a gentleman might well be a recluse and may even exhibit the demeanor of a misanthrope—and he might well be a bit skeptical about grand crusades undertaken in the name of averting great catastrophes—he is never indifferent to those around him or apathetic of their welfare. (While a gentleman might not be greatly aroused by the specter of global warming, it has been observed that he will not neglect to take any measures necessary to ensure the comfort of his hunting hounds.) The MGTOW option also runs the danger of encouraging self-pity, which is the most debilitating indulgence for a man and one that leads to nothing but destruction. We have yet to see where this will go with MGTOW, but they present a serious challenge to our society and the starkest indication of why a new book, like this one, is necessary.

Why This Book Is Different

Today there is still a huge outpouring of advice guides on etiquette generally, with many directed specifically at men and manly behavior. This output attests to a continuing need, though it is not clear that the output meets it adequately. Some offer useful and detailed instructions on important topics: how to fit a suit, pass the dishes at a dinner party, or do battle with a crocodile.[16] By all means, use them for this purpose. Others merely labor the obvious. But above all, what the other books seldom tell you is why: the logic behind the rules. For that is what we need to recover. And the other books will not tell you how that logic is now being tested and how to apply the timeless logic to today's ever-changing circumstances. Instead, when confronting the most critical threats to your manhood nowadays, you will notice that most have become so adulterated with the new politically correct version of manhood as to become useless or worse for men who must grapple with today's crisis of masculinity. They draw back when faced with precisely the difficult matters that now pose the most serious threats to men, and some are little more than litanies of gripes about men from armchair moralizers and opinionated New Age women.

One etiquette book by a prominent author, written specifically for men, bases its strictures on a survey of women. Not surprisingly, it consists mostly of complaints. Concerning the bathroom, for example:

> They [women respondents] got down and dirty about everything from missed aim to shaving stubble in the sink to wet towels on the floor and toothpaste all over

[16] E.g., Mansfield, *Mansfield's Book of Manly Men.*

the counter. This leads to a major truth that men are best off simply accepting: The bathroom is her domain. One man responded about the bathroom, "Like the kitchen, it's all her space, she just loans you some of it." You, the man, are essentially the visitor.[17]

Invoking another cliché, men are charged (perennially) with not listening:

> Repeatedly, female respondents commented on how men appeared to be listening but were not actually paying attention to the conversation.... Almost half the survey comments about communicating had to do with the issue of men not listening. For the sake of peace, harmony, and a better relationship, there is a solution: Take a break from whatever you're focused on, look at the person, and focus just on her and what she is saying.[18]

And finally, the recitation of grievances:

> For all the comments received about annoying behavior, men's bad habits topped the list. These are the things we do, sometimes unconsciously, that are perceived by others as just plain gross.... Men, look in the mirror and see if you recognize any of these habits in yourself:

- adjusting
- nose picking
- spitting
- swearing

---

[17] Peter Post, *Essential Manners for Men*, 2nd ed. (New York: William Morrow, 2012), 26–27.
[18] Post, *Essential Manners*, 44.

⬧ smoking and chewing tobacco

⬧ sloppy dressing

⬧ wearing a hat where they shouldn't[19]

He might have added using contractions in published writing and dangling one at the end of a phrase, which would certainly distress any proper lady.

This author is not writing about etiquette; nor is his book about manliness. It is a prescription for servility, which is always unmanly. It will earn you not respect but contempt. This is not because the grievances are not valid; of course you should be mindful of these things, and in fact, we will discuss some of them in the proper context. But the code of manhood must be based on principles of correct comportment that are valid regardless of current fashions or the vicissitudes of opinion. This author claims to honor such principles, but instead he wants the power to rewrite the rules based on which way the cultural wind is blowing, in this case, as measured by his opinion survey.

To grasp what is wrong with this, we should put ourselves in the place of those who must write the advice books for ladies, and we can see that our author has unchivalrously enticed the ladies into compromising their own rules of comportment. If a lady—and this point is equally valid for a gentleman, so please do pay attention—if a lady has a complaint regarding a habit of her spouse (preferably one at a time—complaints, that is), she should be advised to broach the matter delicately on a personal level with as much patience and love as she can muster. And if she fails at this, the onus is on her to apologize for it. She should not be encouraged to harbor a litany of grievances to be vented to the inquiring eyes and ears of third parties, however

---

[19] Post, *Essential Manners*, 8–9.

anonymously, as if she is part of or organized reform campaign in solidarity with others of her sex aligned against those of her husband. She should not be led to believe that she can, with the aid of the popular press, achieve definitive and permanent justice by seeking to change the nature of her spouse, let alone those of all the other ladies. Achieving accommodation with the imperfections of one's spouse is a lifelong endeavor, and the methods one adopts to address this perennial challenge are far more important than the specific problems themselves.

Not surprisingly, the same author goes on to push the envelope with an extensive list of new duties for men, most of which have little to do with true manhood:

- laundry
- housework
- ironing
- watching the baby
- cooking
- making the bed(s)
- vacuuming
- taking out the garbage
- changing light bulbs
- doing the grocery shopping
- paying the bills
- planning an evening out[20]

We may as well get this matter out of the way right here and now. Unless your wife is incapacitated, and does not have female friends or relatives who can step in and take up the slack, these are not the regular responsibilities of a man, except paying the bills (and I will concede taking out the garbage, when asked, and

---

[20] Post, *Essential Manners*, 14–15.

changing the occasional light bulb). None of this will make you a gentleman; it will make you despised. You have other responsibilities that are more appropriate and important and from which these will only distract you. Aside from earning a living and seeing to other household matters—the maintenance of the dwelling, grounds, car, and the like—you should also concern yourself foremost with the family finances, the moral education of any children who have reached the appropriate age, and upholding your family's welfare and defending its integrity in its relations with representatives of the external world, such as landlords, creditors, lawyers, housebreakers, school administrators, assorted other government officials, and similar annoyances. (And, by the way, a gentleman attends to these matters personally, exercising appropriate discretion. We are sensibly instructed that a true gentleman "is not the sort of chap who would go rushing to the Council for Civil Liberties if his boy is given four sharp cuts across the bum for picking his nose in class.")[21] This is not only what sensible men do; it is also what sensible women expect and respect.

These matters require time and focused attention. If you fail in them because you have been spending your time washing the dishes, others will pay the consequences as well as you, and no one—least of all your wife or children—will thank you for it.

That the great-grandson of the renowned etiquette author Emily Post can reduce the rules of comportment to a list of gripes and elevate the stuff of household spats into the pretense of principle reveals something not only about the degeneration of manners among all of us but in particular about the debilitating

[21] Douglas Sutherland, *The English Gentleman's Child* (Harmondsworth, UK: Penguin Books, 1981), 49.

effects of ideological correctness even among those who should be our authorities on the topic and furnish us with sensible instruction. (*Hrumpph.*)

What all this demonstrates is that it is impossible to offer sound advice on either manners or manhood today without taking into account the larger threats to masculinity.

This book is not written to bemoan the sad state of our times or lament all the impolite and ungentlemanly conduct in the world. Much less is the purpose to nag or scold you into correct behavior. Books lamenting the decline of manliness and bemoaning the loss of gentlemanly behavior are a dime a dozen, and books scolding men, alternatively, for being men and for not being men now proliferate as well.[22] But lamenting and bemoaning, like nagging and scolding, seldom achieve anything. With manhood, while understanding is important, more important is doing, and our emphasis here will be on what you must *do*. The point here is to provide time-tested guidance in becoming the man you will want to be because it will make life more comfortable and fulfilling, both for you and for those around you—not to mention (though I am mentioning it) because it is the code of conduct that has proven itself to make for a society that is stable, prosperous, and free. If you sometimes feel alone in this endeavor and that others are not yet similarly motivated, you must encourage them in this direction, not by nagging or scolding but by your example and your leadership. Subtle applications of pressure can occasionally assist.

---

[22] See Kay Hymowitz, *Manning Up: How the Rise of Women Has Turned Men into Boys* (New York: Basic Books, 2012).

1

THE BASICS

We shall begin with some preparation. It is not necessary that you master all these practices and habits before doing anything else. You may even think that this is all a little silly compared with the weighty matters described above. But be assured that this is not at all the case. "How trifling soever these things may seem, or really be, in themselves," wrote Lord Chesterfield to his son, "they are no longer so, when above half the world thinks them otherwise."[23] Even if you do not accept my advice on all

---

[23] *The Works of Lord Chesterfield: Including Letters to His Son, Etc.* (New York: Harper, 1838), 216. Numerous guidebooks today are at pains to impress upon us that manners are not trivial, and then they proceed to trivialize them. If we are to believe one book (as summarized by an exasperated reader in a review on Amazon.com), a gentleman is a master of banalities: a gentleman never runs out of toilet paper; if a gentleman drinks the last cup of coffee, he makes a new pot; a gentleman always restocks the copy machine with paper; a gentleman uses a coaster. See John Bridges, *How to be a Gentleman: A Contemporary Guide to Common Courtesy* (Nashville: Thomas Nelson, 2012). Even the venerable *Country Life* magazine, long the journal of record for the English squirearchy, in its annual "39 Steps to Being a Modern Gentleman," demands little: A gentleman "never lets

these matters now, if you keep an open mind and consider them, you will eventually realize why they are necessary, and you may decide at some point that these matters are not so trivial as they might seem now.

Most of these points involve instructions that fathers once gave to their sons, apparently with futility because the sons seldom listened. But then they grew up, remembered them, and realized their wisdom, and then imparted them to their own sons, who likewise refused to listen. "When I was seventeen, my father was so stupid, I didn't want to be seen with him in public," runs a possibly apocryphal saying of Mark Twain. "But when I got to be twenty-four, I was amazed at how much the old man had learned in just seven years."

Appearance and Comportment

Both the traditional advice books and the modern ones emphasize a man's appearance and comportment. They do so for a reason. A presentable appearance signals not simply respect to other people but a desire to please them, which is the best default position to demonstrate toward the world, even if you later decide to adopt a different one regarding some individuals within it. Your appearance and comportment are the first impression people have of you, and they color everything else. Pay attention to them. If your father did not teach you how to clean your nails, shine your shoes, press your clothes, remove facial hair, and so forth—or if, more likely, you did not listen to him—get a book with the details or look them up on the Internet. A brief list of other essential

---

a door slam in someone's face" and "turns his mobile to silent at dinner."

habits might include daily washing, grooming, shaving, tooth-brushing, using deodorant, and regular haircuts. I will not be so harsh as to insist, as does one advice book from the nineteenth century, on the superiority of cleaning the teeth with a sponge rather than a brush, nor that all toothpaste is inferior to good "White Castile Soap,"[24] but you get the idea.

Nowadays the Internet makes the specific techniques easy to learn, so there is no excuse for not knowing. I assume that you do not need to be told, as apparently did the readers of a sixteenth-century German advice book, that when attending the most formal gatherings at least, "it is unseemly to blow your nose into the tablecloth."[25] But equivalent horrors abound today. As Oliver Wendell Holmes commented, "In the vulgar herd there is one more than each of us suspects."

Practice good posture. Sit up straight; do not slouch on a chair. Stand up straight with your head held high but without your nose in the air. Regular exercise and adequate sleep are said to contribute to both your appearance and your self-confidence, as well as to your health.

Above all, be positive. You are in control of the situation. Everyone respects a man with a positive and optimistic outlook, rather than a morose and pessimistic one. But avoid all extremes,

[24] Cecil B. Hartley, *The Gentlemen's Book of Etiquette and Manual of Politeness* (Boston: G. W. Cottrell, 1860), 120.

[25] Quoted in Natasha Korda, *Shakespeare's Domestic Economies: Gender and Property in Early Modern England* (Philadelphia: University of Pennsylvania Press, 2002), 127. Even the great Erasmus felt that such matters needed to be addressed: "To blow your nose on your hat or clothing is rustic, and to do so with the arm or elbow befits a tradesman," he wrote; "nor is it much more polite to use the hand, if you immediately smear the snot on your garment."

and learn when it is appropriate to refrain or to mourn. The habitual cheerfulness and familiarity exhibited especially by many Americans can be infectious and charming, at first, but beyond a point it can also become insufferable, and excessive displays of happiness are inappropriate in circumstances where others may be distressed.

Attire

All the advice books, from the sixteenth century to the twenty-first, emphasize a man's clothing, and they do so for good reason. Respectable attire conveys respect to others and therefore commands respect for ourselves. Showing respect is especially important for men, because not doing so can have severe consequences. One advice book from Renaissance Italy observes that "it often happens that duels are fought on no other account but that one man is not treated by another, whom he meets in public, with those marks of respect which are justly his due."[26] Today's equivalents—ghetto shootings, for example—are similarly attributed to one man being "dissed" (that is, "disrespected") by another. And it may be relevant to our topic that such altercations often seem to originate in disputes involving expensive shoes. Some principles do not change with the culture. Respect is essential for a man.

Since the late 1960s, many men seem to have become stuck in a state of arrested sartorial development. Women have suffered less. Yes, many women today also dress like boys, but they have the option of dressing however they like, and they have skillfully

---

[26] Giovanni Della Casa, *Galateo; or, a Treatise on Politeness and Delicacy of Manners*, English ed. (London: J. Dodsley, 1774), 75.

manipulated this freedom to their advantage. Obligatory informality has not given men more options or freedom; it has made them feel self-conscious about looking too much like men, so instead they look like superannuated teenagers. Importantly, overly informal attire is not only adolescent and, at worst, slovenly; it is also androgynous: it blurs the distinction between the sexes. This is never in your interest because it diminishes your distinct status as a man, and most women really do not like it either. They like to feel like women; thus, their obsessive attention to fashion and beauty, even those who deplore this. And, whether they admit it or not, they respect men who look like men.

Living in post-communist Eastern Europe during the 1990s, when people were finally able to buy quality clothing after decades of wearing factory uniforms, I was struck by how elegant the women looked in public while accompanying men still habitually attired in boiler suits more appropriate for the steel mill. By taking over the male functions of providing for the people, communist governments emasculated men and deprived them of their self-respect. A similar trend now operates on a more subtle level in the West, which some believe is being transformed by feminism and similar pressures into a system of soft communism: women dressing with options ranging from elegant to obscene, accompanied by men uniformly presenting themselves as teenage farm hands.

Further, all this may well reflect larger mental impediments to accepting one's entrance into manhood. We have lost most of the rites of passage that in another age marked the beginning of manhood. Higher education today largely just prolongs adolescence. And many men lack fathers and other strong men to encourage them into the transition. Here, as elsewhere, our clothing is symbolic of our larger outlook.

So stop dressing like a little boy and act your age. The standard rule is to "let the dress suit the occasion"[27] and conform your appearance to the company you are with, the occasion, and the conventions of your society. Both underdressing and overdressing can be taken by your company as an insult. "If a gentleman is not absolutely certain as to the dress code for an occasion, he always prefers the risk of being underdressed to that of being overdressed," one modern book suggests. "The former may be interpreted as a simple misunderstanding; the latter suggests conscious premeditation." And what is wrong with premeditation? This is the logic that has ratcheted us down to a level close to nihilism. You need to be a leader and look like one, rather than like a follower, which means you should aim just a little higher than today's norm. If a modest shame is the response of some, this may not be such a bad thing.

Again, we dress to please others, as even the modern gentlemen's manuals emphasize. What they do not tell you is the logic. You may already wear a coat and tie for your job. But is your employer worthy of more respect than your family and friends or the woman in your life? Why? Because they pay your salary? Because they control your livelihood? They have power over you, so they get respect? But your family has no such leverage over you, so you can present yourself to them in a cheap sweatshirt and stained trousers and show them that they do not matter? You may not intend this, but on a subtle level this is precisely the message you are conveying. And in a small way, it makes you a lackey and a coward. Show the same respect to those you profess to love and like as you show to those you fear. They will know it and respect you in return. And then, when you wear a coat

27 Hartley, *Gentlemen's Book of Etiquette*, 116.

and tie to your job, you and others will know that it is because you are showing respect to everyone around you rather than just servility to the boss. Your employer likewise will know it and may begin to regard you as a man to trust with greater responsibility. A puerile journalist once sneered that Prime Minister John Major was "probably the last man left in Britain who wears a tie on Saturdays," which did more to improve my opinion of John Major than any policies adopted by his government.

So get a coat and tie and wear them, even when they are not required. And you should also own at least one conservative, well-made suit. Please spare me the complaints about the cost. You are not required to have it tailored on Saville Row. Many men pay far more for the designer gym shoes and leather jackets that constitute today's casual chic. A high-end clothing store will still assist you to choose and fit your clothes, but in the bargain basements nowadays you are on your own, so a little preparation and research is a good idea. Again, you can go online or to a contemporary advice book for men to learn how to fit a suit and a shirt, tie a tie, press your clothes, and shine your shoes. Once you start to develop this habit, you may well take an interest in it, become determined to do it correctly, and develop your own views on matters of individual discretion. (The fastidious still insist, for example, that "for cuff buttons to be sewn on to a suit purely for show is regarded by many to be as bad as the wearing of a made-up bow tie or keeping their trousers up with a belt instead of braces."[28] *Quelle horreur.*) When you look like a gentleman, you will start to feel like one and want to act the part.

---

[28] Douglas Sutherland, *The English Gentleman Is Dead, Long Live the English Gentleman!* (Edinburgh: Canongate, 1992), 21.

Do not go to the other extreme and become a dandy. A dandy is "a Man whose trade, office and existence consists in the wearing of Clothes," as Thomas Carlyle described him, "so that [while] others dress to live, he lives to dress." Or worse, a fop.[29] An act of nonconformity should have a defensible reason, and a measure of eccentricity can be endearing, if you know how to pull it off without being taken for a buffoon. An elevated appreciation for beauty and aesthetics—whether in women, nature, the arts, or one's own appearance—is part of "the good life" that a gentleman understands. But making aesthetics an end in itself will make you appear shallow. While a man should look neat, well groomed, and professional, a man's dress is always something of a uniform, which conveys an acceptance of duty. That is why a gentleman's suit tends to be limited to gray, dark blue, and (in the country) brown, rather than bright colors. A persistent misconception holds that a first suit should be black, but reliable authorities nowadays regard black suits as appropriate only for waiters and undertakers.

The most formal dress, like black tie and white tie, is the most uniform of all. Unlike a woman, a man is expected to fit in, not stand out. In eighteenth-century Britain, "in any public place one blue- or black-coated gentleman looked and behaved much like another."[30] This is not "boring," nor does it prevent you

[29] Manners columnist Amy Vanderbilt observed years before it became obvious that "it has long been recognized by fashion experts that many innovations in men's clothes—and they are proliferating now—originated among homosexuals and eventually infiltrated into the most conservative circles." Amy Vanderbilt, "Bad Manners in America," *Annals of the American Academy of Political and Social Science* 378 (July 1968): 91.

[30] Paul Langford, "British Politeness and the Progress of Western Manners: An Eighteenth-Century Enigma," *Transactions of the Royal Historical Society* 7 (1997): 59.

from expressing your individuality. Your tie is the one accessory that allows you to make a personal statement, within limits. All this is the visual manifestation of the understatement and self-effacement that epitomizes the gentleman. Self-advertisement is not gentlemanly, and vanity is unmanly. She is permitted to adjust her clothing, check her appearance in a mirror, attend to her hair, and become distraught if something is amiss or becomes disheveled. You may not.

Neither do you need to become a slave to what one nineteenth-century advice writer called "the tyrant fashion," which can become a bad habit in matters other than sartorial. Adopting an accepted, time-honored style of dress is an effective defense against having to succumb to the latest fads, and all the expense and fuss they entail. Moreover, rejecting fads in clothing is good practice for resisting them elsewhere, for changing and frivolous fashions abound in many other realms of life: culture, education, politics, journalism, religion, scholarship, and more. Our most highly educated sophisticates, who rule lofty domains like the arts, the media, academia, and the church, and who flatter themselves that they stand above the vulgarities of the great unwashed, readily jump onto the silliest bandwagons as a substitute for having to exercise their brains. This is not new either: "When the same caprice which gives law to the wardrobe extends itself to the library ... the schools ... religion, it is time that reason should vindicate her rights against the encroachments of folly."[31]

---

[31] Charles Butler, *The American Gentleman* (Philadelphia: Hogan and Thompson, 1836), 46, 50, 51. "The vanity of the great and opulent will ever be effecting new modes in order to increase that notice to which it thinks itself exclusively entitled," he adds. "The scholar and the philosopher are hurried away with the rapidity of the torrent."

Even in casual wear, some little adjustments can make a difference. Get some comfortable trousers that are not blue jeans and walking shoes that are not for the gym. A knit shirt with a collar looks much better than a T-shirt with advertising that turns your chest and back into a public placard. A comfortable, inexpensive sport coat even for casual wear makes clear that you are a man of self-respect and spares the ladies from having to look at your hairy arms and sweaty back and armpits (as well as providing convenient pockets). While you are at it, it may be time to consider dispensing with the tattoos and body piercings and backward baseball caps.

Again, dressing like a child means reverting to the gender neutrality of childhood, and "gender neutrality" is always at the expense of men because it denies the importance of masculinity and masculine achievement. Proper dress conveys not only seriousness and professionalism but also masculinity. It is no accident that the more formal dress becomes, the more sex-specific it is, whereas informal clothing is almost indistinguishable between men and women, or boys and girls. Wearing a coat and tie not only shows respect to others; it also declares your readiness to accept responsibility in general and the specific responsibilities of manhood — responsibilities, incidentally, that women do not have and, feminist claims notwithstanding, do not want.

You will be surprised how differently people treat you. When you enter a shop and the clerks rush up to you, asking, "May I help you?" it will be from a desire to please and serve you rather than a concern that you might be there to steal something. You will be addressed as "sir" with a tone of authenticity. Women will look at you differently, but so will men. People will trust you more and be more willing to entrust you with responsibilities. People are not just treating you differently; they are thinking about you differently.

Most importantly, you will begin to act the part because you will begin to think differently about yourself. This is not hypocrisy because you will not let it become that, by changing your behavior and habits accordingly. If you look like a gentleman, you will be more likely to want to act like one. Your appearance will be a challenge you must live up to (or, because a gentleman always uses correct grammar, up to which you must live). It also does not hurt that good clothing is said to make you look younger, which helps you generally but also in your relations with women.

In fact, your attire says many things about you, and it conveys both to and from you many things, but one thing it gives you is authority.[32] And here is where I will get into serious trouble. For if you look and behave like a gentleman, you acquire the authority to insist that she looks and behaves like a lady.[33]

---

[32] Perhaps germane to our theme of ruling is the principle that length confers authority. As of this writing, a fashion of short winter coats for men seems to reign. At the risk of betraying some kind of complex, I cannot help but wonder if this reflects an erosion of respect for men. Women understand that long skirts command more respect than short ones, and they communicate inviolability, as G. K. Chesterton pointed out when he observed that men who must convey dignity and untouchability also wear gowns, and long ones. "When men wish to be safely impressive, as judges, priests or kings, they do wear skirts, the long, trailing robes of female dignity," he wrote. "The whole world is under petticoat government; for even men wear petticoats when they wish to govern." *What's Wrong with the World* (New York: Dodd, Mead and Company, 1912), 185. It may be significant that none of his examples derive their legitimacy democratically from the people but all claim quasi-sacerdotal authority. The *sans-culottes* changed the game in the French Revolution when they introduced trousers.

[33] See the section on "Appearance and Attire" in part 4.

A GENTLEMAN'S GUIDE

Introductions

In introductions, the lower-ranking person — in age, seniority, professional standing, and the like — is introduced to the higher-ranking person.

A gentleman always shakes hands upon meeting another man for the first time or after a long interruption in their acquaintance. Not to do so constitutes a major insult that should be reserved for the most severe infractions. A handshake should be firm and accompanied by a direct look in the eyes and a smile.

A gentleman shakes hands with a lady only when she offers her hand; he never extends his first. The modern manuals will tell you that rules like this one are now out of date. As is often the case with the modern manuals, you are free to follow their advice provided you are willing to risk a lawsuit for "improper touching" or something worse. When in doubt, it is best to assume the wisdom of the traditional rules.

Kissing the hand of a lady is reserved for older European gentlemen. It is not a tradition among English-speaking men, and is regarded by many as ostentatious, as well as providing more ammunition for those who want to accuse you of sexual something-or-other.

Conversation

A gentleman should readily employ words such as "please," "thank you," "pardon me," and "I'm sorry," and use them profusely, even when they are not strictly required. (A casual "sorry" when it was obviously the other party's fault can be helpful if you wish to be territorial, though the effect is undercut if it sounds the least bit sarcastic.) Adding "sir" or "madam" or "ma'am" is still obligatory in some foreign cultures, and while it has generally been dropped in English, it still impresses, especially when addressing a person older than oneself.

Traditional gentlemen sometimes were reserved and even a touch misanthropic. This is not necessarily a serious fault, and it can have advantages. Remember always the virtue of silence. But it should not be taken to extremes, and the impulse must be overcome when necessary. Permitting others to speak first is virtuous. If you allow them to dominate the conversation, however, your only remedy is to walk away from the tedious. But ignoring others altogether will be interpreted as contempt, which is (usually) not a good idea.

A gentleman must know how to conduct a conversation that is lively and interesting without annoying or offending people and also without being easily offended himself—or at least without doing so needlessly.

A little imagination will supply topics for beginning and continuing a conversation. Avoid talking too much about yourself, and instead ask others about themselves. Try to convey genuine interest in other people, even if you do not feel much of it at first. It can be acquired. When speaking with someone, make eye contact and keep it. Do not be always looking away to see who is entering the room.

Talk about third parties not present should be positive. As one authority describes the double standard: "A female gossip is detestable, but a male gossip is not only detestable but utterly despicable."[34]

Immediately inquiring of new social acquaintances what they "do" demonstrates more than a lack of imagination; it is annoying and offensive. Most people do not identify themselves with

---

[34] Hartley, *Gentlemen's Book of Etiquette*, 311–312.

their livelihood, and they will not appreciate your invitation to compare it with yours. The fact that you have some prestigious or fashionable job does not authorize you to start a new relationship by implicitly establishing your status or superiority. Further, if your own employment signals your position in the world of culture or religion or politics, as is the case for many unattached urban young people nowadays, then introducing it into the conversation violates the next rule. And, by the way, if you do need to be told, you never discuss your own salary or anyone else's.

The traditional advice books urged people to avoid two topics in particular: politics and religion. And the special admonition that "*in the society of ladies*, these topics are best avoided," may have contained more wisdom than was realized even at the time.[35] I must admit that I had trouble understanding this rule at first. Not only are these two of my favorite topics; they are topics on which I have professional training and about which I talk at length for my livelihood. Moreover, in the household where I was raised, we often discussed politics at length during and after dinner, and I later acquired a similar fascination for religion. We also believed that disagreement is healthy and that it can not only encourage civility but also help to refine one's knowledge and understanding. But all that was true because I discussed these matters with family members and others with whom I had already established a relationship of mutual trust. Nevertheless, I must allow that the old advice books were correct, and their wisdom on this point has been lost, with serious consequences.

Both politics and religion are topics on which you should have firm *convictions*, and in the right circumstances you must be prepared to practice and defend those convictions at a high

[35] Hartley, *Gentlemen's Book of Etiquette*, 11 (my emphasis).

cost in terms of personal sacrifice—as the greatest martyrs in both religion and politics have attested. *Opinions*, by contrast, are tedious for everyone. Inquiring gratuitously about people's political opinions or religious beliefs—especially as a prelude to expressing your own (even when solicited, but especially when not)—is a prescription for awkward and unpleasant disagreement or worse.

These are topics that should be discussed with reflection and in depth. When you get to know someone well and develop an in-depth relationship of trust, then such topics can become the basis for long and elevated discussions and friendships. But rushing the matter is not wise.

If you find yourself trapped in a situation where you have become the sounding board for the unsolicited pontifications of an opinionated person, it is best to extricate yourself from the situation as quickly and quietly as possible. Above all, there is no need to engage or try to refute the pronouncements of a bore, which is always a Sisyphean task. Remember the golden rule of conversation: never argue with a fool, because a third person does not know which one is the fool. If you cannot withdraw gracefully, then you are permitted subtle, purely visual expressions of boredom like a suppressed yawn. If the hint is not received, you may depart with a brusque "Please excuse me."

Develop the habit of using standard, grammatical English, and avoid any kind of specialized, esoteric, or fashionable vocabulary. Whether it is highbrow or lowbrow, the effect is to exclude some people from the conversation, and it suggests that you are addressing an exclusive circle of the *cognoscenti*. This includes both professional jargon that you have acquired because of your education or business and the trendy slang that you have acquired from social contexts, the media, or "the street." Even phrases that might seem natural to you can come across as lazy or construed as pretentious. Acronyms and initials that signify well-known proper names (NASA, AA) are more forgivable than those that substitute for ordinary words or that are used as words in their own right, which is lazy. Not everyone knows that "ROI" means "return on investment," "POS" means "point of service," or "DUI" means "driving under the influence" (of whom?). Most people might figure out after a few seconds that "ETA" means "estimated time of arrival" and "ER" means "emergency room," but they should not have to. If "TMI" means "too much information," do not add to the overload by expecting people to know this. Whatever the intention, lazy jargon of this kind places you in a position of superiority over the unfortunate ignoramus who must ask what you are talking about.

Likewise, never assume that another person is familiar with the latest cool expressions, whatever the media is presenting as the latest trend, or the current buzz on social media: "GOAT," "snatched," "YOLO," "periodt," and the like. These will not impress anyone over the age of about eighteen and, if used by a person above that age, will likely elicit contempt by those under it. If you talk like an overgrown teenager, that is just how people will think of you.

Avoid trite and clever and clichéd expressions of any kind. "Have a good one," has become ubiquitous, but this does not make it standard English quite yet. Likewise, "I'm outta here," may generate its own expressions of relief and be taken as welcome news just by virtue of being uttered, but that hardly makes it worth adopting as a habit. And as one book advises, "Nothing is in worse taste in society than to repeat the witticisms or remarks of another person as if they were your own."[36] This is true

---

[36] Hartley, *Gentlemen's Book of Etiquette*, 308.

even when you are not pretending otherwise. Whoever coined the phrase "bells and whistles" to refer to fancy but unnecessary computer features was indeed clever, but repeating it to people who have heard it even once before, let alone dozens of times, will come across as the opposite: a person too dim-witted to devise his own humor. ("Crunching numbers" is another that has worn thin.) What is acceptable or cool among your intimate circle is not necessarily appropriate for everyone else. People should not be required to check the *Urban Dictionary* to decipher what you are saying. Try to *avoid* demonstrating that you are *au courant* of the latest expressions and trends.

And this includes expressions like "*au courant.*" At one time, knowledge of foreign expressions could be assumed among the educated, and they can still be appropriate in writing, but they should be used in conversation only among those with whom you have an established relationship. Most people are not impressed. Even less so when you invoke foreign phrases for no good purpose. You might use terms, as I have above, such as *arriviste* and *cognoscenti*—especially if you are one—among people whom you can be certain will know these terms. "*Adios, amigos*" adds nothing, when you can simply say "goodbye."

The general principle is that you want to make yourself understood by all people, of whatever age, class, educational attainment, opinion, creed, nationality, or cultural background.

Using Americanisms—or what were once seen as Americanisms, though many have become widely mimicked and almost universal English—is off-putting to many people and can present you as shallow: "And I'm, like …" "And then she's, like …" Slow down and employ clear terms to say what you mean: "I said," or "I was thinking," and so forth. Slowing your speech will also help to avoid inelegant fillers such as "you know" and "uhm."

Showing a slight skepticism or gentle annoyance toward the latest buzzwords can also signal that you are not easily swayed by fads and that you will need to be persuaded, and can help command respect. If you must employ "best practices" in your work, do not leave the impression that this term in itself renders others' practices not so good. A few years ago, everything suddenly needed to be "robust." As of this writing, it is "bespoke." When you read this, it will be something else. Whatever it is, find another word.

This shows that you are a man of substance and thought, rather than one who simply follows the latest fad. In fact, one word that is especially appropriate to our subject that you might force yourself to use when referring to any male over the age of eighteen is "man" — in preference to "guy," "dude," "bloke," "bro," "geezer," and the like. After all, is there something wrong with this word? Or perhaps a fear of the responsibilities that accompany it? After a few repetitions, it becomes easier.[37]

Finally, nothing will more quickly win for you the label of vulgar than talking loudly in public places and inflicting your private conversation on others in the restaurant, train, or street. Unfortunately, the mobile telephone has exacerbated this problem and multiplied the opportunities for being the cause of it. Once associated especially with Americans abroad, this fault has now become endemic to English-speakers generally and other Westerners. Keep your voice down, and take the telephone outside.

---

[37] *Mea culpa*: In writing this book, I found myself having to go through and locate all the instances where I had inadvertently and habitually used "gender-neutral" terms and replace them with what were at one time the standard masculine ones. Perhaps naively, I assume the language police will permit me this indulgence in a book for and about men.

Speaking of noise, you should at least be aware of Lord Chesterfield's diatribe against laughter, including "the disagreeable noise that it makes, and the shocking distortion of the face that it occasions." He believed that a gentleman should indeed exhibit "true wit," which "never yet made any body laugh," but quiet wit and raucous laughter were two different things. "There is nothing so illiberal, and so ill bred, as audible laughter."[38] While I do not insist on this prohibition, laughter is always annoying when displayed in the presence of people who are excluded from the joke.

VULGARITY

Speaking of vulgar, as you might guess, a gentleman is not a potty mouth. He does not use profanities casually, if at all. Nothing breaches the rule of both giving and commanding respect so quickly—or needlessly. Even other men who hardly consider themselves delicate will instinctually think less of you and consign you to the category of a lowlife, or at least they will want to avoid association with you. Women, of course, will be insulted and repelled. If nothing else, vulgarity breaches the rule of aiming for elegant speech and writing. The English language is rich enough to convey almost any sentiment, including the most negative ones, without resorting to gratuitous irrelevancies such as distasteful bodily eliminations, crude sexual acts, or offensive religious blasphemies. This is true regardless of whether your aim is anger or humor, or simply the result of habit.

The only real purpose of vulgarity is to shock, and as with a narcotic, the effect lessens with use. If a gentleman uses profanities at all, it is only after careful and deliberate calculation, when

---

[38] *Works of Lord Chesterfield*, 180.

it is *extremely* important. Vulgarity can shock effectively only when you have a reputation for never using it and for behavior that is otherwise impeccable. Vulgarity is the nuclear option: once you use it, you can never use it again. Make sure it is of the highest importance and utterly unexpected.

Writing

At one time, a gentleman was expected to have elegant handwriting. In the days of computers, there is less opportunity to use this, but the occasions when you can—such as handwritten notes of gratitude, apology, or affection—make it all the more impressive. I must admit that when I encountered students who could take time-pressured essay examinations, of all things, using a florid hand and do it well, I was truly impressed—not only by the writing itself, but also by the presence of mind that it demonstrated.

Handwritten letters, notes, and cards also demonstrate thoughtfulness on important occasions: expressing gratitude, apologies, congratulations, condolences, friendship, or love. Full-length letters are especially likely to get attention and win admiration.

In any case, a gentleman should be able to write good English when occasion serves, and writing must be more correct and formal than speaking. For this reason, good writing also encourages better speaking. This requires basic knowledge of spelling, grammar, and usage, while avoiding informalities, colloquialisms, and contractions.

As compensation, writing allows you more precision, nuance, and elegance than speech. You can labor longer to find the right word or phrase, avoid awkwardness and hesitation, and catch *faux pas*. In writing, you can draft and redraft, which enables you to reduce verbosity and redundancy and employ a richer vocabulary, especially stronger verbs, rather than the ubiquitous "have" and "get" that we all use in everyday speech. You can also take certain liberties not permissible in speech: foreign phrases, literary allusions, and especially apt (and short) quotations. Your writing acquires authority if your point has been made by more eminent people. Here, too, the effect works only when used in moderation and as appropriate to your purpose. Overuse is ostentatious.

When appropriate, writing is also a more effective and safer method of expressing disagreement, annoyance, and anger than speaking. Spoken anger is rarely effective in conveying one's message and then only when there has been opportunity for adequate preparation. Often it is harmful for him who is expressing it and leads to further animosity and regrets. It is best to hold your tongue at the moment of injury and then compose your grievances with moderation, subtlety, nuance, measurement, and effect. This also allows the target of your anger the opportunity for reflection and the option of an apology or amends or, if you turn out to be in the wrong, correction without humiliating either of you. On the other hand, all these advantages of writing will also render more effective your determination, once you have exhausted the alternatives, to twist the knife.

The Romans had a saying that should be the inscribed motto of every college and university — and is for some: *Docendo disco, scribendo cogito*. I learn by teaching, I think by writing.

As we will see later, writing is also an effective method of courting a woman.

These advantages of writing also make the advent of e-mail, if used correctly, a welcome development. It has revived the art of letter writing — sort of. E-mail etiquette is a topic on which a large literature can now readily be found on the Internet, and for the basic and obvious rules, there is no harm in consulting it. But most of it concerns rules for business and professional settings, and a gentleman should be correct in his personal correspondence as well, including friends, acquaintances, family members, and others.

Here, too, it is a good habit to use correct grammar, spelling, and the like in composing even routine e-mail messages. First, it sets you apart from the adolescent practitioners of "OMG," "LOL," and "NOYB." Second, precision in grammar and spelling also shows respect to the recipient. Like comely attire, it tells them that they are important enough for you to take the trouble to address them correctly. It therefore encourages other e-mail etiquette, such as composing messages that are clear and concise and complete, thus avoiding having to repeat yourself in later messages, to the annoyance of all. No one likes receiving unnecessary e-mail, and succinctly saying all that needs to be said the first time is appreciated by people whose time is limited, which describes all of us. Some believe that short messages are preferable to omnibus compilations, and that different subjects should be treated in separate messages, appropriately labeled in the subject line, which is indeed a helpful courtesy. But perhaps most important, e-mail is a medium that is highly conducive to misunderstandings and quarrels. Waiting and reflecting and redrafting before pushing the Send button is always a good idea. I seldom send even the most routine messages without drafting the message once, waiting for at least a short interval, and then redrafting it at least one more time before sending. And when I fail to do this, I almost always regret it.

Public Speaking

As we have said, a gentleman is never the first to grab the microphone, and he is never keen to display himself in public in any way. Nevertheless, occasions will arise when he is called upon to speak publicly, and often this means persuasively. That is, he will be required to speak in a way that conveys important information or convinces people of some important point, perhaps leading to some specific action. This can be daunting, and apparently the most widely shared phobia in our society is the fear of addressing an audience.

The concept of "rhetoric" is often in disrepute, both in history and in our own time. It has long been associated with deception, the ability to "make the worse argument appear the better," which is more properly called *sophistry*, though distinguishing the two is part of the training. Aristotle said that "there is a thin line between virtue and vice, and a sophist can easily turn one into the other." More recently, the term "rhetoric" has also been debased to mean empty words covering an absence of substance. ("That's just a lot of rhetoric.")

But at one time it was considered essential to a gentleman's education, just as it was to that of the citizen. In the days before the printing press and the Internet, when active citizenship was exclusively a male privilege and duty, the ability to speak publicly without fear and with effectiveness and elegance was the mark of manhood because there was no other way to be an active citizen but to stand up in the assembly or market square and deliver a speech. In fact, the practice and skill have long been associated with political freedom. A political theorist once observed that the preferred medium of communication in monarchies is whispering, whereas in republics and democracies it is public address.[39]

---

[39] Michael Walzer, *Regicide and Revolution* (Cambridge: Cambridge University Press, 1974), 28.

A GENTLEMAN'S GUIDE

This is why the arts of rhetoric and elocution have been valued throughout history and among the most successful and admired periods of our civilization, from the oratory of the Greeks and Romans, through the public speeches of the Renaissance and the sermons of the Reformation, to (for better or worse) the rabble-rousers of the great modern revolutions in England, America, France, and beyond.

Manuals are available that can help you prepare grand speeches, formal lectures, or simply informal talks. As with writing, this is where your knowledge of basic rules of grammar and usage becomes essential and even more conspicuous. And as in writing, be concise, keep sentences and paragraphs short, and aim for a rich vocabulary without becoming grandiloquent.

But perhaps the most important rule is simply to *take the time and take your time*: first, take the time to prepare your talk carefully, and then, when you deliver it, take the time to do so slowly and clearly. The Greco-Roman rule was to memorize an entire speech, and you should aim for this ideal, if possible. Some people — including employers and others who can determine your advancement — value as a major asset the ability to speak extemporaneously. In the British House of Commons to this day, if a speaker uses notes or even glances at the back of his hand, he invites a derisive chorus from the opposition benches: "Rea-ding! Rea-ding!" Otherwise, notes or a text, depending on how skillfully you handle them, can create either a disaster or a successful speech. It has been said that bad speakers write out their entire speeches on paper, that good ones speak extemporaneously from notes, and that great ones write out their entire speeches on paper.

The art of rhetoric also teaches you how to recognize logical fallacies, which is why logic was closely associated with rhetoric and grammar in the education of a gentleman. The three constitute the "trivium," which every educated man was expected to know and which is not trivial. Logical reasoning and facility with words is especially useful for a gentleman if he is likely to be attacked verbally with slanders or libels—which he is if he ever says or does anything of substance. If he does not want to duke it out with fisticuffs each time he is insulted, the skill and power to respond in kind is essential. "If the worthiness of eloquence may move us … with a word to win cities and whole countries," wrote Thomas Wilson in his treatise *The Art of Rhetoric* (1553), "what greater gain may we have than without bloodshed to achieve a conquest?"[40]

Going Out

In most circumstances, a gentleman allows a lady to go first, holds doors for her, helps her with her coat and with her chair, and walks on the curb side when accompanying her on the street. He allows a lady into the taxi first and then, barring heavy traffic, goes around to the other door, so that she does not have to slide across the taxi.

All these rules, however, have always been subject to qualification according to circumstances, and recent changes in the circumstances have qualified them even more severely. For example, a gentleman precedes the lady if there is likely to be any difficulty or danger. He precedes her going up the stairs, but follows her down the stairs. Technological and other changes

---

[40] *The Arte of Rhetorique, for the use of all suche as are studious of Eloquence, sette forth in English* (London: Richardus Graftonus, 1553), front matter (n.p.). Language has been modernized.

have long made it easier for ladies to attend to matters such as doors themselves, before the gentleman can, so oftentimes the offer or intention is enough.

More than that, however, is that changes in ideological fashion on the part of some ladies have rendered it positively hazardous for a gentleman to attend to these matters without risking a scolding. The fact that other ladies do not accept these changes in ideological fashion makes it equally hazardous for the gentlemen *not* to attend to these matters, at the risk of an unpleasant glare. Further, the prerogative of all ladies to accept or reject the changes in ideological fashion as they please and the fact that some please to do so inconsistently at different moments in the same afternoon places all men in a state of uncertainty and confusion. In these circumstances, the gesture must suffice, and if the ladies who place themselves on the cutting edge of ideological fashion are offended, then the best you can do is smile and tip your hat (an argument in favor of being one of the few remaining gentlemen who still wears one) in silence.[41]

---

[41] The most nuanced guide I have seen on the details of these matters is "The Anatomy of Etiquette," published in *Esquire Etiquette: A Guide to Business, Sports, and Social Conduct* (Sydney: Angus and Robertson, 1954), especially the sections entitled "Your Hands" and "Your Feet," parts of which I am summarizing. For example, he sensibly qualifies the rule about walking next to the curb by adding "when you can do it gracefully": "It is better, however, to walk on the inside than to convert a simple stroll into a ballet: don't cross back and forth behind her or be forever running around end just to get into position. The rule is supposed to be for her comfort and her safety; she finds nothing comfortable about talking to a whirling dervish, and nothing particularly safe about leading the way through traffic while you're running around her heels."

Further consequences of the ideological changes are that some ingrained and traditional habits of gentlemanly behavior nowadays can put you in a potentially troubling position. If you habitually allow women to enter first through doorways or on exiting elevators, you may inadvertently find yourself in a position of following a woman you do not know. You must not permit this to happen.

In boxes at the opera, ballet, or theater (which, of course, a gentleman patronizes), which are typically allocated four seats to a box, the gentlemen take the two seats at the rear of the box and allow the ladies to occupy the two seats at the front, even when the couples are not acquainted with one another. This allows the ladies not only to see but also, and far more important, to be seen. The fact that some people (or computers) who sell tickets nowadays do not know this rule and will happily sell you the two seats in the front does not justify you in displacing another gentleman's lady by occupying a front seat, displaying yourself and your black evening jacket to the audience while denying them the delightful sight of the lady and her beautiful dress.

Published in 1954, however, this guide hesitates to apply the rules to "modern women hipped on 'independence,'" and already he is making the shift from ensuring that the woman benefits from the rules to allowing her to make and remake them at whim: "Don't expect her to be consistent," he warns. "Just because she opened the last three doors, foiling all your efforts to play the gallant, don't be surprised if she waits expectantly before yon magic-eye door. Your job is to be ready and willing at every door, and to let her specific conduct be your guide at each one." The novel assumption is that the woman is, essentially by definition, always right, means that "the gesture is what counts with an independent dame."

Meals

Etiquette manuals are popularly associated with rules governing table manners. This, too, is no accident. Eating is one of our most sociable activities. It is the one thing no one enjoys doing alone, not even reclusive and unsociable people, as indicated by the word *convivial*, signifying the value of eating and drinking in company. "The true pleasures of a gentleman are, [*sic*] those of the table," said Lord Chesterfield, "but within the bounds of moderation."[42]

In itself, eating is an animal activity. Civilized societies refine and elevate it as much as possible, to the point where it becomes the occasion for an assortment of critical social functions, from educating children, to celebrating life events and achievements, to sacralizing religious observances, to formalizing business agreements and international treaties. Offering and sharing food not only creates companionship but also builds trust. It is harder to injure or betray a man whose hospitality you have accepted. Take it seriously, but beware: "In no field of endeavor is the social mountaineer more likely to fall into a crevasse than over the dinner table."[43]

Again, the standard rules on how to behave during meals are readily available in the traditional and modern etiquette manuals, which are generally reliable. "You ought to take care ... if possible, not to spit during that time; or, if you are under a necessity of doing it, it ought to be done in some decent manner," a guidebook from the Renaissance advises. "It is also very indecent to rub your teeth with the tablecloth or napkin, and

---

[42] *Works of Lord Chesterfield*, 149.
[43] Sutherland, *English Gentleman Is Dead*, 60.

to endeavor to pick them with your finger is more so."[44] Further strictures to bear in mind, in the event that the gaps in your upbringing have left you unaware of them, include:

- "If in the leaves of your salad, or in a plate of fruit you find a worm or insect, pass your plate to the waiter, without any comment, and he will bring you another." Or at least he will remove the creature.
- "Never put bones, or the seeds of fruit upon the tablecloth."[45]

If you require more up-to-date rules, they can quickly be found on the Internet. One quick caveat: nowadays it has become standard practice to ask guests beforehand if there are particular foods they cannot eat and attempt to accommodate them. This should not become the occasion for a disquisition for the benefit of the entire company about one's views on the treatment of animals or the specifics of one's health, let alone one's taste preferences. If you cannot or do not wish to eat a particular item, it should be quietly declined, if possible with a brief explanation to the host, but not to the other guests.

A man also traditionally courts a woman over a meal and similar occasions. She, in turn, may reciprocate by cooking for you and others, which even today is a favorite method used by women to express affection. If she expresses disdain for this, you might ask yourself why.

This is carried into the family, where the man traditionally sits at the head of the table. Some men today are reluctant to assume this role, and it is also no accident that the proliferation of single-mother homes has been accompanied with the decline

---

[44] Della Casa, *Galateo*, 178–179.
[45] Hartley, *Gentlemen's Book of Etiquette*, 53, 55.

of family meals, increased reliance on fast food and convenience food, and obesity and other forms of slovenly behavior. Once the man is eliminated from the family—at least when he is forcibly or voluntarily removed, rather than retaining his place of honor through death—the "family" no longer really exists, and one indicator of this is the rapid loss of the family meal. One result is children who are not only fat but frequently obnoxious.

So here again it is your job to preserve the feast as a bastion of civilization. Minimize the times you are "too busy" for a meal together, and make it the exception rather than the rule. During courtship, buy or cook her meals, make substantial conversation, linger over meals at leisure, and pay the bill without discussion. In domestic life, indulge her in matters such as the ordering of the kitchen, which she may wish to claim as her domain, and buying items to enhance the preparation of meals and the dining environment. You are not necessarily required to "help" in the kitchen, and some women prefer that you do not. You can open and pour the wine. Far more important is to enjoy the time together over meals and show gratitude for her effort. There is a reason why real estate agents insist that the two most important items in selling a house are the kitchen and the bathroom: that is what the women first notice. When you and she are ready for it—and certainly with the appearance of children—meals also present a good opportunity for you to get in a moment of your own propaganda, when appropriate, in the form of a short prayer.

Gratuities

This is a difficult one. Leaving tips has become almost obligatory in the Western world, and the practice seems to be spreading and the percentage formula ratcheting ever upward. It is tempered, at least theoretically, because the formula excludes added taxation and tipping the proprietor of the establishment. In parts of the world, tipping is still not required at all, but pressure is increasing. Some people have tried to resist the trend on the principle that it is condescending and demeaning, and some people are uncomfortable treating others as servants. Workers should receive a standard wage from their employer and not be required to hustle for basic remuneration. If you adopt this noble attitude and put it into practice, you will likely be able to visit each establishment only once, for the reality is that some people in countries such as the United States depend on it for their livelihood. It is also considered acceptable to set the amount based on the performance of the job, though the rest of us do not have our pay reduced each time we have an off day or when the volume of work prevents us from attending to every detail as we would prefer. At one time, even some employers discouraged the practice, because if the customer is paying the serving staff directly, then the question arises of whom precisely they work for, the employer or the customer. Some consider it a form of bribery, which it can be. We are not encouraged to tip policemen or judges, after all, though other methods are available to achieve the desired ends.

In some countries, you are not required to leave anything, and in others you can simply round off the bill. In such places, leaving too much, usually by foreigners, can even be resented by the locals, both customers who fear the obligation and even the workers, who fear that their wages will be reduced accordingly. I have been reprimanded, for example, in Central and Eastern Europe, where I witnessed friends, on a bill equivalent to, say, $8.86, leaving $9.00 or even $8.90. Try getting away with that in Manhattan.

Overtipping is considered by some to be vulgar and ostentatious, though "the suspicion that this is put about by the parsimonious under the excuse that it is ungentlemanly is probably very well-founded."[46]

So the choice is yours. Service to others is not inherently demeaning. We all serve others in our various capacities, both personal and professional, or we should. But being paid extra for it voluntarily does seem to be inherently a practice of the well-to-do toward those lower on the income scale, if not the social one.

Vices

Gentlemen have traditionally had their share of vices, however much they tried to hide, excuse, or elevate them. Whether it was putting down bets at the steeplechase or keeping mistresses, gentlemen (or those posing as such) have not only *not* always been paragons of virtue; they have developed their own distinctive forms of vice. Sublimating one's pleasures with the pretense of refinement does seem to provide some assistance in keeping both the vices themselves and the harm to others under control. There is also the view of some that "little good comes from society chasing men's vices underground where they can't be moderated."

It's not surprising that so many men today treat alcohol, gambling, and tobacco like a fourteen-year-old boy who just found the key to daddy's liquor cabinet. Which is part of the reason why men need their vices—at least a little. Men need to ... learn what is too much and what is just right.[47]

---

[46] Sutherland, *English Gentleman Is Dead*, 63.

[47] Miniter, *Ultimate Man's Survival Guide*, locs. 2521–2525, 2528–2529, Kindle. Mark Twain "knew he'd gone too far when his wife

Still, the tendency for the indulgences of gentlemen to take more benign forms from those of the *hoi polloi* has had an unfortunately misleading effect. Remember that one of your responsibilities as a gentleman is to set a good example, because if you are successful in achieving that "respect" that we and others have placed at the heart of gentlemanly status, then what you do is likely to be imitated. It is our civilizational tragedy that vices that seem (and I stress *seem*) innocuous when practiced among the affluent and educated can become highly toxic when they spread to the poor and uneducated. Casual sex and bearing children outside marriage first became fashionable among the sophisticated, but it eventually led to ghettos of fatherless homes that are responsible for most poverty, violent crime, and other social ills — as well as the demonization of men, something that should certainly interest you. Social drinking seems harmless but also contributes to public drunkenness, binge drinking, and associated dissipation, especially among the young and poor. Recreational drug use among the affluent has culminated in the epidemics of crack cocaine and other hard drugs, with the hideous violence that accompanies them. Further, I am tempted to include on the list fashionable atheism and substitute religions such as socialism, which first gained traction among the gin-and-tonic set and which rationalize comfy middle-class welfare services in affluent countries but produce little besides instability, stagnation, and repression in poor ones. So remember that your leadership may be for ill if it is not for good when you are tempted to believe that your peccadillos are "not hurting anyone."

---

told him so," Miniter continues, "as women once moderated men, instead of emasculating them."

TOBACCO

Cigarette smoking has gone from the fashionable to the illegal. Nowadays it can also be grounds for social ostracism, to the point where, in some venues, smokers are ignominiously consigned to cubicles resembling public fishbowls. In the process, the stigma has become surrounded by self-righteousness that can be insufferable. Still, the fact is that it has always been recognized as a habit that is unpleasant for many and unhealthy for all and one that must be subject to strict rules. From the start, there have been those who wished to eradicate the habit altogether, starting with no less a figure than King James I of England in the early seventeenth century. "One must never smoke in a public place, where ladies are or might be," one book suggests. "One must never smoke when anybody shows an objection to it."[48] So there you have it. If even the traditional books support the anti-smoking campaigners, then I fear that they do have the weight of authority on their side, though not a license to be obnoxious. If you find yourself in a country where public smoking is still accepted, and you or your companions find it intolerable, you must use your discretion. If the local custom is against you, you may have no choice but to depart yourself. In settings where the rules are ambiguous—for example, in some European countries, where it is formally forbidden in public establishments but still widely practiced—*politely* asking the offender to refrain is acceptable. It is not acceptable to start fanning the smoke away or coughing ostentatiously, let alone yelling, *"No smoking!"* from across the café. If a polite request is not honored, a pointed but silent relocation to another table or seat is permitted.

---

[48] Hartley, *Gentlemen's Book of Etiquette*, 303–304.

At the least, it is best to ask permission, smoke outdoors where possible, and always at a distance from children and pregnant women. But naturally the best course is simply never to start, which means avoiding the first cigarette, which can be the start of the addiction.

Here too, cigar and pipe smoking are seen as more refined for a reason. Not only are these the products of decades of tradition and somewhat less unhealthy, but they are also more likely to be enjoyed in an appropriate specific location, where the occasion for offense is minimal. For some, the tradition of following a meal with cigars and brandy (after the ladies have withdrawn), or tobacco shops, where men still go to enjoy cigars and pipes (and escape the company of women) still holds a certain nostalgic appeal as the image of the gentlemanly ideal. Like traditional men's barber shops, they even appear to be making a comeback. But such establishments are also being invaded by women, so really the main point is defeated, and all you have remaining is the unhealthy habit.

ALCOHOL

Taking intoxicants to the point of intoxication and loss of faculties and judgment is never consistent with being a gentleman. A gentleman is always in control of himself.

Yes, at one time, a knowledge of claret or port was perceived as one of the essential trappings of a gentleman, but even total abstinence is a perfectly legitimate option. If you do decide to drink alcohol, there are reasons why some choices were traditionally associated with refinement and others with dissipation, though, of course, any version will readily assist you in making a fool of yourself. Drinking in solitude is always unwise. "Social drinking" may be a euphemism, but conviviality is always preferable to isolation. Drinking in a pub or tavern at least should make it an occasional event rather than a habit and puts you in the company of others who may be able to help you know when you have had enough. Wine is part of a culture, and good wine is usually drunk with food and in company, which mitigates its intoxicating effects. Thomas Jefferson said that "no nation is drunken where wine is cheap; and none sober, where the dearness of wine substitutes ardent spirits as the common beverage." (Though, if you must be told, as some books in the past evidently assumed that you must, it is generally taken as ungentlemanly to knock back a full glass of wine in one gulp.)[49] Some gentlemen used to adopt the practice, common in wine cultures, of allowing their older children to drink diluted wine in small quantities. Nowadays even the French, who epitomize this culture of wine, have experienced the ravages of binge drinking among adolescents, but evidence suggests that this results more from the breakdown of the family than their traditional oenological obsession.

Beer was at one time encouraged as an alternative to gin and other spirits, which were the equivalent to crack cocaine in the eighteenth century. Expense can also help to mitigate overindulgence. The trend toward single-malt whiskies, whose prices as well as quality necessitate that they be sipped, rather than blends, which were knocked back over ice or mixed, is perhaps welcome. The contrary trend toward cheap alcohol mixed with sweeteners is certainly unhealthy and has probably arisen to meet demand from women and even children. I am tempted, therefore, to tell you to "drink like a man." If you must adulterate your beer

---

[49] Hartley, *Gentlemen's Book of Etiquette*, 63.

with sugar or use fruit juices and soft drinks to make you spirits palatable, your body may be telling you that you should not be drinking. If you cannot learn to appreciate or afford good beer, quality wine, or a fine cognac, then you may be drinking for the wrong reason.

A basic knowledge of dinner wine and other quality alcohols is not difficult to acquire, but there is no need to go overboard and become a snob. For wines, one generally orders a dry or semi-dry wine with dinner, unless the lady expresses a preference for something else. The rule about red wine with red meat and white with lighter meats and fish is not rigid. The point is that the flavor of the wine should not overwhelm that of the food, but you can vary it. French or Italian wines are not necessarily any better than those from California, Australia, South Africa, Chile, or elsewhere, especially at the high end, but at the lower price ranges, they tend to be safer. An inexpensive white Bordeaux or Beaujolais Villages will be quite drinkable, whereas a cheap California plonk with some clever name like the Belching Bunny written in bright pink letters could be inviting disaster. French and other European wines identified by the vineyard are generally of a higher quality than those identified by the region, which, in turn, are better than those identified by the grape, but this generalization has many exceptions. A lowly "vin de table," which is what the locals who make it all probably drink, can be perfectly agreeable.

A few cautions to disarm the snobs and avoid making a fool of yourself: one should not "mix wines" of high quality, but everyday wines are likely to be a mixture already and present no impediment. If a waiter, upon opening the bottle, presents you with the cork to sniff, simply take the cork and place it on the table; this is a pointless affectation. The ritual of pouring a small amount into the gentleman's glass before filling the lady's allows you to take in any taste of the cork and to test that the wine has not gone sour. It is not for you to assess its quality, so there is no need to humiliate yourself with elaborate pretenses that you are satisfied with the flavor — or worse, by sending a perfectly sound bottle back to the cellar. I have it on good authority that the waiter will simply return with the same bottle in hand.

As for sweet dessert wines, fizzy wines ("Champagne"), and the like, no real guidelines are necessary, and you can leave these to others to choose. After all, an excessive attention even to quality beverages is not healthy, and alcohol should not be the subject of obsessive discussion.

Finally, as we are also sensibly instructed by knowledgeable authorities from the past, "Do not put your glass upside down on the table to signify that you do not wish to drink any more."[50] If you think such gaucherie is the stuff of legend, consider the modern equivalent of placing one's hand over the glass. One gentleman recounts his own home life, where any guest guilty of this offense "was in for an awakening, when the butler, on my father's orders, continued to pour the wine over the offender's hand until it was removed." It is plausible to believe that the butler complied, given that the accepted practice of simply allowing your glass to be filled and not drinking more than you wish allowed butlers one of their traditional perquisites of polishing off the leftovers.[51]

In closing, we should remember again a larger reason to be suspicious of intoxicants of all kinds. Frederick Douglass illustrates the reasons in his *Autobiography*, where he explains why he

50   Hartley, *Gentlemen's Book of Etiquette*, 57.
51   Sutherland, *English Gentleman's Child*, 75.

decided to forgo alcohol altogether. During his years on a Maryland plantation, the slaves were given a week off at Christmas, during which time they were liberally supplied with alcohol at the master's expense. The reasons are obvious: to prevent thoughts of escape or insurrection. Intoxication is more than unattractive, unhealthy, and wasteful; it is also a kind of bondage. To be a free man and a leader requires self-control. (A similar principle applies to other indulgences, as we will see in the section on sex.)

GAMBLING

Here is another vice that has forms associated with sophistication and others associated with dissipation. Any form can ruin your life. Some arguably encourage manly virtues such as risk-taking and camaraderie, while others are simply lonely and contemptible. The worst forms, those based on blood sports such as cockfighting, have mostly been banned, and for reasons that bear on the gentlemanly ideal. They were outlawed under pressure from the Puritans, according to the historian T. B. Macaulay, not so much because of the cruelty they inflicted on the animals, as because of the pleasure they gave to the spectators. This was not quite true, but the principle is still valid. There is something unhealthy about taking enjoyment at the sight of blood and violence, let alone making money on it.

Games such as slot machines are solitary and require no skill, which is why they are almost universally regarded as neither manly nor sociable, but only sad.

More refined versions requiring skill, principally card games, developed as the recreational accompaniment of financial speculation — itself a form of gambling, with arguably both positive and negative forms and consequences of its own. In fact, this occasioned the founding of the famous "gentlemen's clubs" of St James's Street in London, themselves the precursors of modern casinos. While dissipation was certainly a feature of these establishments, to the point of becoming an object of public ridicule, a certain code of honor also operated. Winning was not the most important quality. More respected was the willingness to risk and lose large sums of money with equanimity and without loss of composure. And faithfully paying one's debts was, of course, a visible virtue, because being creditworthy and trustworthy is essential to both a gentleman and a prosperous society.

The lesson here for the modern gentleman, and hopefully the moderate gambler, is that the inevitable loss of money and time should always be expected and written off as a cost of socializing and entertainment. If you lose enough to push yourself beyond a dignified comportment, you are over your head.

Etc.

If you were ever tempted to use illegal drugs, now is the time to stop it. I am not just moralizing, and I am not particularly even concerned about the health effects or the fact that they are illegal, so there is no point in telling me why some are harmless and should be legal. I am also not concerned with the politics. Whatever the merits of legalization, they cannot negate the destructive effects of use. First, any addiction or intoxication is debilitating and weakens your strength, judgment, and morals. Even if you resist addiction, illegal drugs are part of a culture that is inherently unseemly, even if it is fashionable. There is no reason to take them other than intoxication, and you have or should find more constructive ways to spend your time and money. Yes, Sherlock Holmes had both cocaine and opium habits, but Conan Doyle never presented this as anything other than a weakness, and a sordid one at that.

Getting About

Various methods of moving himself from one place to another can offer special challenges to the dignity and composure of a gentlemen. Correct comportment is not likely to be the first concern to the man whose main aim is to reach a destination. Be aware that your conduct is often even more noticed and more susceptible to scrutiny when you travel than when you are in other public places and act accordingly.

Transport sometimes entails special rules because it is often undertaken as part of a group, or at least in interaction with others. When people are grouped into vehicles in large numbers and then temporarily cut off from the rest of civilization, the authorities in those vehicles become temporary rulers and police, with legal authority over everyone in it. Captains of ships, even civilian ones, traditionally exercised this authority and still do, and pilots of planes can now have a similar status. But even the driver of a car can be held responsible for what happens both outside and inside it. The fact that the persons in these positions of authority are most likely to be men means that they are all the more likely to be given responsibility for the conduct and misconduct of others and to be held responsible if anyone does something incorrect. If you find yourself in any of these capacities, you must, of course, observe the codes of not only professional but personal conduct, and even if you are only a passenger, your conduct may be scrutinized and regulated by people whom you might otherwise think have no authority to control your behavior or pass judgment on it.

Further, even private transportation vehicles can become the occasion for intervention by other authorities and unexpected responsibility by you. Stumbling on the sidewalk seldom leads to being stopped and interrogated by police, whereas a similar misstep when driving a car could well have this result. Police who lack the authority to arbitrarily stop and search your person on the street without "probable cause" are more likely to do so with your car or baggage.

All these conveyances are now governed by recently devised codes of etiquette, easily found on the Internet, though honestly, their rules are, for the most part, obvious. As always, we will limit ourselves to matters of special concern to gentlemen.

WALKING

The most healthful, and, in many ways, the most pleasant, form of transportation is the most basic. "Now shall I walk / Or shall I ride?" asked the poet W. H. Davies. "'Ride,' Pleasure said; / 'Walk,' Joy replied." Not only are the fuel requirements minimal, but using the vehicle can itself actually help minimize repair bills. Walking keeps you most in touch with your surroundings, which in itself encourages gentlemanly comportment. It is also conducive to thought and even extended reflection, as writers and philosophers have long attested. It can be a time to reflect, develop ideas, work out problems, think out theories, compose poems, and so forth. The Romans had a saying, *solvitur ambulando*: it is solved by walking. "I can only meditate when I am walking," philosopher Jean-Jacques Rousseau apparently claimed. "When I stop, I cease to think." Given that his *pensées* were the main inspiration behind the French Revolution, it might have been more salubrious for everyone if somebody had offered him a lift.

Gentlemen are traditionally avid walkers in the countryside, often for recreation on footpaths and trails. And here you can go all out with your new self-image, donning a tweed jacket and cap, a pair of Wellington boots, and, if you really want to make a spectacle of yourself, a wool tie and knee breeches. The fact that others spend far more fuss and money adorning themselves in the colorful synthetic gear once thought necessary only for expeditions atop Kilimanjaro justifies your indulgence in pointed understatement, which can be another mark of a gentleman.

But even on city streets and in parks, a gentleman will walk not only for pleasure but also as part of his daily routine. The only environment where it is neither practical nor pleasurable—and it is an expanding one, taking over vast stretches of our planet—is in the dreary roadscapes of suburbia.

Walking is also the form of transport still most governed by simple, old-fashioned human interaction—that is to say, etiquette. I would like to say that walking remains outside the general strictures described above about government regulation of transportation, but I fear that this may no longer be true. Of course, informal rules and principles have long governed places such as crowded city streets, and some of my counterparts among the impromptu etiquette experts have now developed more elaborate codes. This is generally to the good, though, as elsewhere, the more zealous of the experts are not content to stop there but want to call in the state gendarmerie to supplement their flexible informal rules with rigid legal statutes. One such codification, from the East Village of New York City, would require all pedestrians to obtain a permit from the Department of Pedestrian Etiquette. The proposal is apparently facetious, at least for now, though everyone who cites it seems to lament this fact. Infractions, quoted *verbatim*, include:

- blocking the sidewalk or any public area in a large group or just standing like an idiot in the middle of pedestrian traffic
- walking too slowly with more than one person spread across the sidewalk
- stopping abruptly without stepping off to the side
- blocking ped[estrian] traffic to stare up at the Very Tall Buildings or to clump in a group to look at maps
- walking with your face in a map or mobile device
- stopping on a bike path with a big group to take pictures of squirrels[52]

Like any expansion of government power (always for the greater public good, of course), this one would have the added benefit of creating a convenient patronage machine for the otherwise altruistic reformers, providing a clientele of beneficiaries who would help to implement the new powers, ensconce the reformers in positions of official authority, and then expect to be rewarded. The inevitable fees and fines would transfer income from the ill-favored but privileged pedestrian oppressor class to the downtrodden proletariat of "Underground Artists, Community Art Spaces," and so on.

Regulating pedestrian traffic always presents certain problems. As elsewhere, inconsiderate practices do abound and must be discouraged. (The above list is a selection of only the reformers' more legitimate grievances.) On the other hand, pedestrians are not generally a threat to anyone's safety sufficient to warrant

[52] Sarah Goodyear, "The 'Department of Pedestrian Etiquette' Targets Clueless NYC Walkers," Bloomberg CityLab, Bloomberg, https://www.citylab.com/transportation/2015/07/the-department-of-pedestrian-etiquette-targets-clueless-nyc-walkers/398384/.

police intervention, unenforced traditional "jaywalking" laws notwithstanding. Moreover, the tourist group that blocks the path with their dawdling has its counterpart in the lone native who races, runs, or jogs down the sidewalk at high speed, indifferent to what lies in his path. To "walk fast in the streets ... is a mark of vulgarity, ill-befitting the character of a gentleman,"[53] wrote Lord Chesterfield. "Hurry, bustle, and agitation, [sic] are the never-failing symptoms of a weak and frivolous mind."[54] To my knowledge, he had no views regarding tourist groups. None of this, I hasten to add, necessarily merits incarceration.

The above litany suggests that this conflict is frequently one of the town dwellers, often as individuals, versus tourists and other visitors, often in groups. This indicates that the conflict is actually part of a problem of wider significance: the crowd. A lone pedestrian is generally fully aware of his surroundings and ready to make accommodation to the needs and peccadillos of others. He will readily apologize for an accidental bump or near miss, even when it is not strictly his fault. Give that individual a companion, and much of his attention is immediately diverted from his surroundings to his conversation, accommodating or impressing his companion, and so forth. He quickly becomes semi-oblivious and more than semi-indifferent to what is happening beyond the pair. Add a second companion, and the effect increases considerably. Add two more, and you have a group. Add ten, and you have a crowd — a crowd with its own dynamics both internal and external that become more important to each individual than the welfare of others on the street. The

---

[53] *Lord Chesterfield's Principles of Politeness, and the Polite Philosopher* (Gainsborough: Morley, 1792), 55.

[54] *Works of Lord Chesterfield*, 153.

crowd has a destination or some other collective purpose that takes priority over all else. It develops a group solidarity that values others in the group more than those outside it and creates an impromptu loyalty to that group to the exclusion of others. It dominates its space and the space around it on the street. It demands *de facto* priority, because the individual who encounters the crowd cannot expect the crowd to give him precedence, even when it would be much faster for him to go first, for example, through a doorway or onto a train. So he must accommodate himself to the movement of the crowd, give precedence to the crowd, circumnavigate the crowd, and so forth, rather than expect the crowd to defer to him. As anyone knows who has resided in a tourist destination, this can be extremely annoying, especially when the crowd is perceived as aliens trespassing on one's home territory.

I have no clear solution for this problem, beyond the obvious but ineffectual one of exhorting everyone to patience and politeness. Indeed, if I did have a solution I would have succeeded where great philosophers have failed, for I would have solved one of the great conundrums of political thought and civilization itself, which is how to control the mob, a problem far more serious than impeding New Yorkers from getting themselves to the Met (to be charitable about their likely destination). All this validates James Madison's famous quip that, "had every Athenian citizen been a Socrates, every Athenian assembly would still have been a mob." I am not suggesting that every group of Chinese tourists is ready to grab pitchforks and torches and run rampant through the streets of Manhattan, though it sounds as if they may inspire some New York natives to fantasies of similar measures. Certainly public authorities are more justified in formally regulating organized groups than individuals, and I suppose the rest of us should always make sure they realize this. Here again, we should also resist the temptation to regulate other people ourselves with more than a polite request, a hard stare, or a cold shoulder.

BICYCLES (AND THE LIKE)

For a gentleman, a bicycle can be one of the joys of urban life, and the closest substitute for that lost symbol of rural gentlemanly status: the horse. While bicycling, like horseback riding, can be a form of recreation and exercise, it is especially gratifying — and more symbolic of gentlemanly status — if you can incorporate it into your daily routine as a useful means of getting about. Like walking, riding a bicycle is healthful and turns transportation from a chore into a pleasure while avoiding the stress of waiting through traffic lights and traffic jams, as well as incurring car expenses. With a little skill, you can usually repair the bicycle yourself and avoid dependence on professional mechanics or your brother-in-law.

Some people respond that it substitutes the stress of physical danger while riding on roads and streets, but this can be minimized if you avoid excessive speed, plan your route, look for bike lanes, and stand ready to claim your status as a semi-pedestrian by retreating onto the sidewalk at the first sign of trouble. So, a bicycle, with some self-imposed restraint, gives you the best of all worlds. You can pretend to the status of a vehicle, with a rightful place on the road and the equal of the cars — or, since you will never achieve this equality, you can instantly return to the status of a human.

As always, all this privilege brings with it responsibilities, especially because it can lead to some problems, as you can probably imagine. Bicyclists may have the best of all worlds, but they are also resented by all the others in those worlds, sometimes with reason. Cars find them annoying, but so do persons on foot. Riders perennially complain, with good reason, about the discourtesies and dangers to which they are subjected by cars. Yet they then turn around (not literally, and not all of them) and inflict similar terrors on pedestrians, either when crossing the roads or on sidewalks. In some jurisdictions it is illegal for adults to ride a bicycle on the sidewalk, and while at times you must do it to stay alive, remember that it is a privilege and not a right. The pedestrians *always* have precedence. Not only must you not plow into them; you must not race past them at high speed—even while arrogantly dinging your bell—striking terror into them or forcing them to freeze in their tracks in the hope that you will swerve clear at the last minute, especially the elderly. In fact, you must not inconvenience them in any way. It is not up to them to move out of your way; it is up to you to stay out of theirs. When the route is crowded or blocked, slow down and drag your feet on the pavement to show that you are not a threat and, if necessary, simply dismount. Yes, it does require considerable patience and presence of mind to willingly break one's momentum, but controlling the irrational impulse to move ever "forward" and achieve open-ended "progress" for its own sake, is a virtue in itself and one applicable to other spheres of life.

Some jurisdictions try to solve (i.e., regulate) this dilemma by imposing "designated" bicycle lanes in otherwise pedestrian areas such as sidewalks and parks. This indeed is a cause for lamentation because, unlike bike lanes on roads, which make sense because roads are already government-regulated space, this transforms the sidewalks and parks from places ruled by face-to-face human interaction into government-regulated terrain, enforced ultimately by police and courts. This amounts to a victory for the bullies among the bicycle riders and further endangers pedestrians by giving the bikers a feeling of entitlement to run down any unfortunate walker who inadvertently strays into what he may not realize has now been designated a public highway. Bicyclists who regard this official recognition of "their space" as a triumph should beware. Perhaps predictably, some people are now taking the logical next step and calling for bicycles to be registered like cars and riders to be licensed like drivers. Fees and taxes will surely follow. Police regulating more areas of our lives is the consequence of ignoring and discarding the rules of gentlemanly behavior.

Fortunately, traditional principles of deference still seem to operate on walking trails and footpaths, where hikers and horses both have priority over bicycles. Horses have priority over walkers and hikers, who have precedence over bicycles. This might seem strange, given that horses are bigger and stronger than humans, but they are also more difficult to control in small spaces and to predict, so this rule is for the safety of people as much as anyone. When passing a pedestrian or another bicycle going in the same direction, saying something audible, such as "passing" or "on your left," is more personal and less jarring than dinging your bell, which should be reserved for those delicious instances when righteous indignation is truly warranted.

Newer vehicles with ambiguous status, such as skateboards, roller skates, scooters (electric and otherwise, with seats or not), along with various other hybrid devices, have become a source of annoyance to both drivers and pedestrians and present similar problems, precisely because appropriate rules have not yet been devised. In the meantime, we should all temper our annoyance with the realization that these are preferable to more cars everywhere, and if we go back to the days when Toad and Rat were knocked over by the novelty of a passing "motorcar," we might recall that at one time it was cars that were the major source of annoyance to others, and often still are. But if we do not want state functionaries taking control of every inch of our lives, the price is not only exercising some courtesy but also encouraging—and if necessary, shaming, pressuring, and so forth—our fellow riders to do likewise.

Cars

Quite an elaborate code of conduct now regulates how people should behave both inside moving cars and as they move them about in relation to one another. Most of it consists of obvious strictures on obeying the rules of the road, refraining from back-seat driving, and so forth. Within the car, orders of precedence have also developed stipulating who sits where, depending on age, sex, status in the family or firm, and so forth. Again, such codes as can readily be found on the Internet are fairly straight-forward and obvious, and I will refrain from elaborating here, but this gem of sociological protocol from the Etiquette School in California is worth sharing:

> How couples seat themselves when traveling together is an indication of their social class. When two men and two women of the working class are traveling together, the two men sit in the front seats of the car, and the women take the back seats. In the middle class, one couple sits up front, and the other couple sits in the back. Upper-class people choose a different arrangement. The woman of one couple sits up front with the male driver of the other

couple, while her companion sits with the driver's female partner in the back seat. The man in the back seat defers to the woman by giving her the seat of honor—passenger side rear. The assumption of this seating arrangement is that a couple spends a good deal of time talking with one another. A mixed seating arrangement encourages cross-conversation between couples, thus fulfilling the purpose of getting together—to exchange scintillating conversation, news, and ideas.[55]

So, once again, etiquette gives us all social mobility and the means to be rich and upper class, at least for the length of a car ride.

Externally, the car is a highly unsociable form of transportation and therefore a special challenge for a gentleman to maintain his composure. On the street, once again, it is usually not so difficult for the individual to maintain, at least for the brief time of his ambulation, the outward comportment of a gentleman. Even in the absence of good breeding, the pressure of face-to-face interaction and fear of disapproval generally encourages "situational awareness" and keeps most of us in line. A gentleman on the street, or even more so in the countryside, is therefore generally the epitome of decorum. Here again, he will readily defer precedence to others, overlook their infractions, and be the first to offer an apology even when it is not strictly necessary. Put that same gentleman behind the wheel of a car, and then commit the most insignificant transgression of the rules of the road—as he chooses to interpret them at any given moment—and you

---

[55] Found in "Car Etiquette—Tips on Seating a Woman and Couples in a Passenger Car," EzineArticles, https://ezinearticles. com/?Car-Etiquette---Tips-on-Seating-a-Woman-and-Couples -in-a-Passenger-Car&id=4786036.

will likely unleash a lengthy torrent of uncharitable vituperation expressed in the most ungentlemanly language, impugning the other driver's character, intelligence, legitimacy, the chastity of his wife, and more. It is much easier not only to insult a man but also to descend to the level of a barbarian when you are not looking him in the face and when you do not have to face the consequences of your words. So perhaps the search for alternative forms of transportation to the car may have effects even more salubrious than conserving fossil fuels.

TRAINS, BUSES, AND AIRPLANES

As air travel, like train travel before it, has become less elegant and more a matter of herding passengers around on uncomfortable "cattle cars," friction among passengers and with the travel companies has grown acute, and an extensive literature now addresses such momentous matters as tray tables, armrests, backrests, excusing oneself gracefully from a window seat, and the order of precedence for exiting. Assuming that a gentleman is as likely as anyone to be traveling in the least expensive and most uncomfortable section of the plane, he should do what he can to minimize not only his own discomfort but what he might cause to others, as well as the indignation he expresses to the personnel of the airline or train company who must perform sometimes impossible tasks and implement distasteful procedures. Rather than weigh in on such pressing questions as whether a traveler has the "right" to recline his plane seat and under what circumstances, I will simply refer the reader to the extensive literature on the Internet and urge that he form his own views.

2

PASTIMES, SOCIAL, AND CIVIC LIFE

Music and Dancing

Traditionally one of the social graces expected of a gentleman was skill at dancing. Playing a musical instrument was an added asset, though one reserved for intimate circles of family and friends and not necessarily to be displayed in public for anything so vulgar as material reward—let alone to be imposed unrequested in public on random passersby as an excuse for begging on streetcorners, at train stations, and so forth. In general, the piano, violin, and guitar, or its predecessor the lute, are the instruments most likely to be called for spontaneously on social occasions.

As for dancing, some moralists objected because they believed, correctly, that dancing leads to sex, but others thought it was better to refine (i.e., regulate) it, ostensibly for aesthetic reasons but also to keep the sexual element under control. There is indeed an erotic element to most dance. "Opera" glasses, invariably placed in performance halls where ballets are also performed, are not there to help you hear the aria better. If you know the principles, you can better judge for yourself.

The purpose of most dance is to showcase the beauty of the woman. The man is really an accessory; he serves as the frame for which she is the picture. (This attitude is helpful, in fact, whenever you plan to accompany a lady in public on a social occasion.) That is why women like dancing and are attracted to men who can do it well. Even the feminists are not immune from this principle, though their novel "modern dance" often dispenses with the man altogether, while at the same time managing to make the sexual display as explicit as possible. In traditional dance, as compensation for his secondary role, the man gets to lead. This assures the woman that he will make the decisions and allows him to keep some control over how much she can display herself. The old forms, such as classical ballet and country or "contra" dancing, kept the sexual element under the regulation of formal rules. This is why you should acquire the skill of more formal dancing, such as waltz, ballroom, and swing. Women enjoy it and, again, are impressed by men who can do it. It also provides a more dignified alternative to the dancing—uninhibited to the point of nihilistic, and at once highly sexualized and largely androgynous—that has dominated the young since the advent of rock music.

In fact, this might be a good place to mention popular music, which has become obsessed with two fundamental human drives that are absolute poison for the modern man: uninhibited sex and uninhibited rebellion—often in combination.[56] As a young man, you will likely be tempted by both these narcotics, temptations

---

[56] One example illustrates the motif: A prim and proper teacher is instructing a classroom of young children. Some young men break into the room, wiggling their bodies accompanied by loud, raucous music. The prim and proper teacher is shocked and appalled, but soon she starts wiggling too. At first, the children are shocked by the teacher's behavior, but then they join in. Needless to say, no further instruction takes place. All

that tend to emerge at the same stage of life and naturally reinforce each other. It is therefore natural that you would be attracted to music that expresses these primal urges. You may admire other young men who wiggle on videos, surrounded by women in various states of undress, shouting angry thoughts, in obscene lyrics, about all that is wrong with the world. Aside from giving you a rush of emotional ecstasy, none of this accomplishes anything other than to offer two deadly weapons to people who will readily use them against you. Later we will discuss why unregulated sex and militant rebelliousness "empower" everyone *except* heterosexual men, who end up as the primary targets. We will also discuss forms of music whose unexpected virtues include serving as an alternative to all this.

Sports

On the principle of "a sound mind in a sound body," a gentleman should be proficient at sports. It provides fitness and health and also instills self-confidence, fortitude, endurance, teamwork, and indeed, sportsmanship. Sports were also the traditional background training for military service, which is partly why sports are traditionally the bastion of men and masculinity. Fitness is important for women as well, but not to the absurd lengths to which is carried today, especially with professionalization, meaning really politicization. Not only do most women not share the interest of almost all men in sports, but professional women's competitions negate a basic principle of sports because it is based on the practice of excluding the best competitors so that inferior

---

this is depicted as the triumph of some admirable principle and a happy ending to the little drama.

ones can win. Contact sports, created for the strongest men, are also dangerous for young girls, among whom they produce many serious injuries and health problems, but no one is allowed to discuss that.

Here, too, there are reasons why some sports are traditionally associated with gentlemanliness more than others, and it is not mere snobbery. Sports that are conducive to participation rather than spectatorship should take priority. Access to a gymnasium is the best all-around resource, and a swimming pool is also advisable.

I will not discuss gym etiquette, another realm for laboring the obvious. It is only worth mentioning that some commercial gyms have become so feminized that they cover the walls with dickeybird-watching moral admonitions to PC goodness, and an alarm bell posted conspicuously on the wall sounds if you are perceived as acting too much like a man. Since sex-segregated gyms are now illegal—even though they make everyone more comfortable—you might look for an old facility that is run down and dirty, which the women will avoid.

If you can incorporate walking or bicycle riding into your daily routine, you will gain benefits, psychological as well as physical, that are lost by today's overdependence on cars. Sports such as tennis, squash, and racquetball require some skill, but once acquired they can be profitably played for a lifetime and well into old age. By contrast, the various forms of football are all beneficial for youth but quickly become unplayable with age. An old adage says that soccer is a gentleman's game played by louts, and rugby is a lout's game played by gentlemen. American football started as a gentleman's game, in the more exclusive colleges and universities, but has now become classless and professionalized, like everything else in America. But the point is still the same, because after a certain age, all these sports become largely matters for spectators. It is usually easier to find a place and the equipment necessary to play basketball, volleyball, and the like. Baseball and cricket are also major spectator sports, but both maintain a healthy link with participation because they contain subtleties that appeal to the mind and are lost on those who lack an intimate familiarity with the game, so it is difficult to enjoy watching them without some experience playing. Baseball's lack of connection with institutions of higher learning does not make it any less intellectual or gentlemanly—if anything, the opposite—but this has spared it the hyper-commercialization of other sports. If you are a gentleman of South Asian or West Indian origin, cricket is also a satisfying means of humiliating the English by beating them at their own game, and while a gentleman does not harbor such petty motivations, I am told it is good fun. Cricket also connects you with South Asian gentlemen of other nations and religions against whom you might otherwise be tempted to harbor disagreeable prejudices. In South Asia, Europe, and no doubt other regions, both cricket and soccer also serve as helpful alternatives to warfare.

Most of the organized team sports mentioned above developed because urbanizing economies increasingly lacked the outlets that country men had previously enjoyed for exercising their masculinity physically through their livelihoods. But while urban sports are perfectly legitimate and beneficial, you should also consider rural sports. There are reasons why the traditional gentry were associated with hunting (a.k.a. shooting), "the hunt" (i.e., foxes), fishing, riding, and so forth. Falconry may not be among your priorities, but it is very much alive. Later came mountain climbing, and nowadays hiking and backpacking, kayaking and canoeing, and others that serve urbanites exclusively. All these connect you with nature and encourage an ethic of reverence and conservation, though some do so in ways that are healthier than others. The more traditional sports were connected with private land, and being a gentleman was traditionally associated with owning land, to the point where the term "country gentleman" became natural. A gentleman should have reverence for the land and, if you are fortunate enough to own some, a sense of stewardship. Land is a trust to be respected, cultivated, improved, and passed on to the next generation. It should also be made available, where possible and appropriate, for the benefit of one's neighbors and the public, by allowing walking, riding, hunting (shooting), hunting (foxes), and fishing. This ethic is partly responsible for the beauties of the English countryside, where the private rights of each landowner were considered sacred but where rights-of-way allowed public access on foot and bridal paths and for foxhunting (now foolishly illegal). Thanks to the legal industry and landowners' fear of being sued, American equivalents in such regions as New England and Virginia are now mostly covered with "No trespassing" signs.

By contrast, and thanks to some zealous gentlemen gathered in groups such as the Sierra Club, some outdoor sports for urban elites have become an extension of nature worship and the political ideology of environmentalism. According to this ethic, protection of the land is entrusted not to private landowners — some of whom may well have been expropriated and evicted to create the nature preserve — but to paid rangers and other kinds of police and civil servants.

For similar reasons, older gentlemen should consider gardening and encourage their wives in this pursuit. Not only is it healthy, both physically and mentally, but it contributes to civility and civilization. "Rural scenes, of almost every kind, are delightful to the mind of man," observes one advice book.[57] Young men today naturally prefer the more rugged and rustic enjoyments of nature described above. But nature alone and untamed wilderness, which many today revere almost as a religion, while indeed beautiful, is also savage and cruel. It may be no accident that the word for "nature" is feminine in most languages. The masculine God placed us in a garden. The garden tames nature and captures and cultivates its beauty, while controlling its violence, all by applying the skill of the human hand. The garden is an important symbol of civilized life that a gentleman must preserve.

Firearms

At one time, one mark of a gentlemen was the practice and privilege of carrying a sidearm. When the Japanese samurai were forced to give up their exclusive right to carry swords, it marked the end of their status and really their existence and of Japan's feudal society. At some point, this started to have unfortunate consequences, with the proliferation of dynastic and clan warfare, duels, and other private violence. Gradually these practices were suppressed and superseded by lawsuits, which undoubtedly did help to diminish the level of violence and have long been hailed as an advancement in civilization. In retrospect, it is not clear that this improvement was not without some unintended and unfortunate consequences of its own. It greatly diminished the role of private citizens and householders — that is, men — as protectors of themselves, their homes and families, and our freedom. Instead, it substituted (and forced us all to pay) a professional gendarmerie that acquired a near monopoly over the means of

---

[57] Butler, *American Gentleman*, 266.

force and that has become increasingly authoritarian, bureaucratic, and subject to political manipulation—that is, a positive threat to our freedom. It also greatly augmented the power of lawyers, who have become our professional surrogate citizens, and judges, who are rapidly becoming our *de facto* rulers.

At the same time, the invention of firearms also contributed greatly to the democratization of warfare and therefore of society, as Alexis de Tocqueville observed. This is another reason a gentleman should encourage their safe and skillful use.

Whether you own and carry a firearm is a matter of circumstances and choice, as it is still legal in many locations. At the least, a gentleman should know how to use a pistol, a shotgun, and a rifle proficiently and safely. Sport shooting is good training and effective in relieving stress. Shooting targets, especially moving ones, will help you achieve proficiency. Shooting game also has a spiritual dimension. It connects you with nature and teaches you to respect her. If you have moral qualms about killing animals, then overcoming them is a good defense against moral arrogance and can help inculcate the lesson that being human, and especially a man, inescapably involves showing gratitude and asking forgiveness. (In some cultures, women are not permitted to kill even domestic animals.) Even if most of your meat comes from the supermarket, it is good to be reminded that someone must do the dirty work.

It has even been said, with approval and some justice, that "the impression generally given of the average English gentleman is of a man who, on getting up in the morning, goes over to the window to draw the curtains and remarks, 'What a perfectly lovely day! I must go out and kill something.'"[58] For some men,

---

[58] Sutherland, *English Gentleman Is Dead*, 65.

a gun is his most prized possession. "There is a tradition handed down from generation to generation that the things that one should never lend, even to a friend, are one's gun, one's horse, and one's wife, in that order."[59]

Fencing is also good exercise and relieves stress. You may not share the insistence of Sir Thomas Elyot, author of the sixteenth-century classic *Book Named the Governour*, that "shooting the long bow is principal of all other exercises," but no doubt you can find alternatives.

Military Service

At one time, being a gentleman was inseparable from service to one's country, as expressed in the phrase, "an officer and a gentleman." Not serving in arms was something a man had to explain. "Every man thinks meanly of himself for not having been a soldier," observed Samuel Johnson. Indeed, the fact that most men do not serve nowadays has had a seriously debilitating effect on the status of all men as well as on their self-confidence and self-respect. Subtly, it has also eroded the freedom of all of us.

The phrase quoted above also reflects the fact that the status of officer was at one time the military counterpart to status in the aristocracy, because originally they were the same, and the distinction has survived even after the decline of aristocracy or in countries that do not have one. Alexis de Tocqueville may even have discovered one reason why modern republican states seem more warlike than the old aristocracies. Under aristocracy,

---

[59] Douglas Sutherland, *The English Gentleman's Good Shooting Guide* (London: Michael Joseph, 1989), 15.

an officer's rank was assured by his social status, whereas in a republic, officers need wars in order to earn promotion.

In the newly republican polities of Renaissance Italy, Cromwellian England, and early America, service in a militia came to be considered inseparable from citizenship. "Every citizen [should] be a soldier," Thomas Jefferson and others of his time believed. "This was the case with the Greeks and Romans, and must be that of every free state."[60]

This ideal has been eroded by several factors. The end of conscription in most countries and the rise of professional armies has helped sever the link between the soldier and the citizen—or at least created the illusion that the link is severed. Not only the man but the citizen derived a certain moral and civic authority from his willingness to fight and die for the defense and freedom of his country, which could then be claimed against the privileges of the upper classes, who were increasingly finding ways to opt out of the duty.

Armies have also become highly bureaucratic, turning many soldiers into functionaries and allowing many of the functions to be filled by women, which, of course, further undermines their necessarily masculine quality. Naturally this trend has been exacerbated by feminism, with the highly ironic result that the military has become one of our most feminized institutions. It can be positively hostile to men, with regular scandals concerning "sexual harassment," soldiers emasculated and humiliated, and military command politicized and cheapened, by being ordered to wear high heels, and other oddities.

---

[60] From a letter to James Monroe in 1813, quoted in *Corks and Curls*, 95 (1983): 222.

On the principle that men naturally avoid any institution dominated by women, the result is that men now avoid the military, and so there is a perennial recruiting shortfall. Instead, some disaffected men join underground militias. Still, you should be prepared to assume the role of soldier if required—or alternatively, be prepared to demonstrate physical and moral courage, along with the corresponding hardships and sacrifices, in other ways. Training in sports and firearms is good preparation, including outdoor sports, which teach survival techniques. There is no need to go overboard and start stockpiling freeze-dried food, but the basic skills and habits of self-reliance can increase your self-confidence. Military life instills discipline, sacrifice, endurance, leadership, obedience, and, of course, strength and courage. If you do not get them in the services, you should learn them elsewhere in the company of men.

Church

A gentleman is a moral leader. This will become especially apparent when you have children. Mothers provide physical care and emotional nurturance, as well as early discipline. But if you cannot provide moral instruction to your children as they come of age, then you are just a second-rate mother, which means you have no real purpose and are disposable.

Church is the logical institution for exercising this moral responsibility, with the added benefit that churches are a great place to meet good people (including good women, to be described shortly), whose company will help you to become a better gentleman (by introducing you to good women, among other ways) and who will appreciate and encourage your efforts to be one. Church is where people have committed themselves to at least trying or pretending to be good, which is really the same thing as being good. But this is only the beginning, and believe it or not, churches do still have other useful functions. (And we will attend to the matter of religious belief later.)

Yet men no longer go to church very much, and when they do go, they are often not engaged in what is going on. This is mostly because churches have become dominated by women. Any church where the presiding clergyperson is a woman is almost certainly more of a political outfit than a real church and is best avoided, unless you wish to be harangued about your proclivity for domestic violence and rape. Even in the more traditional churches, where the priest or pastor is still a man nominally, he is most likely being controlled by his wife and the other women in the congregation. Often these are young women who have received little instruction on the doctrines they are supposed to be practicing and on how churches are supposed to operate, let alone how they themselves are expected to behave. Women have the time and leisure to lead most of the activities, and they may even be divorced and sexually active and nurture values and vices directly antithetical to the church's doctrines. With women already outnumbering men in the pews, the clergy are terrified of further losing membership, which leads them to further abdicate leadership in favor of the women and trendy doctrines of gender equality. The result is that churches have become little more than social clubs that are largely hostile to men.

Churches today, therefore, offer little in the way of moral instruction. If you are afraid of going to church because you tremble at the thought that the preacher might peer down at you from the pulpit and threaten fire and brimstone for all the wickedness that he knows you are committing, then you are in for an awakening, and not the kind usually associated with religious revivals. Because the clergy are terrified of offending their congregation, especially on the matter of sex, they seldom preach on sexual morality or subjects such as divorce, cohabitation, adultery, and so forth. In fact, sin generally has become off-limits as a subject for exhortation from the pulpit. It is far more common to hear the preacher haranguing the congregation about their racism, sexism, misogyny, homophobia, intolerance, inclusiveness, diversity, lack thereof, and so forth. Even those churches that claim to be "Bible-believing" and try to avoid the politics have reduced religion largely to a form of psychotherapy.

Yet churches are still critical institutions. It is no accident that leadership roles were traditionally reserved for men, and women were expected to be silent. Now it is precisely the opposite. Weak as both the churches and the men in them have become, they can and must be reinvigorated together.

Like the family, the church serves as an alternative authority to the state, and therefore its authority is a potential limit on the power of the state, which otherwise becomes tyrannical. It is in your interest to strengthen churches and exercise leadership within them. Under your leadership, churches can again be institutions to lead the community and defend families and the freedom of all of us. The churches are also still seen as the traditional guardians of sexual morality, but, since few still exercise this role, it is critical that you learn how to take the lead in enforcing it.

So do not just go to church; be a leader there. Fortunately, this is not difficult. Offer to serve as an usher or read the Bible lesson or the collective prayer. Traditionally, we are told, a gentleman reads the lesson "with great gusto, particularly such passages as deal with fornication."[61] Join the vestry, parish council, or whatever body serves effectively as a kind of board of directors. If meetings on weighty subjects are held, attend them. If there is a "Men's Ministry," join it, but beware. Such groups can often be indoctrination sessions on how bad men are. Since part of the church's role generally is to tell us how bad we all are, this can seem appropriate, so take the criticisms to heart. But this can also camouflage some more insidious and unwholesome tendencies, such as trying to convince you that the solution to your shortcomings is for you to become more like a woman. You do not have to take this. Many men are indeed often bad, as we all are, but make sure that you understand *why* we are bad. Today it is less likely to be because we are not enough like women than because we are too much so. Be aware, too, that many, probably most, men who participate in these men's ministries, though they will verbally flagellate themselves on cue over their own reprehensible masculinity, will secretly be grumbling about the control of their lives, and their church, by younger, opinionated women. And, by the way, so will the good women in the congregation, so there may be room to slip in some unorthodox views (politically unorthodox, you understand).

Knowing the basics of the Bible is also one mark of an educated man. If you have no prior familiarity, it is not as difficult to acquire as you may think, and understanding the references when someone mentions them marks you as a man of depth. It is especially impressive if you can quote famous passages or even short familiar phrases from the King James Version or the Douay-Rheims Bible — the ones with the archaic language: "And

---

[61] Douglas Sutherland, *The English Gentleman's Wife* (Harmondsworth: Penguin, 1981), 58.

thou shalt say unto Pharoah, *Thus saith the Lord*" (Exod. 4:22). These phrases and events have been part of the shared knowledge of educated people for centuries, and regardless of your beliefs, knowing them will do more than almost anything to help make you feel as if you are a member of that group.

Above all, show respect to beliefs that you may not understand or accept, suspend your impulse to pass judgments and share your own opinions, and set an example in these matters for your own children or any others present. One major role of religion is to help you understand—and this is a good way to start understanding it—that fixed principles and convictions that have been shared and tested for centuries, even if you do not fully understand them right away, usually contain more wisdom than your own momentary and transitory opinions.

If all the God stuff does not sound like your cup of tea right away, for now it is not necessary that you even believe it. (We will explain later why you should.)

Philanthropy

We have already suggested that a gentleman's sense of duty often requires that he execute his responsibilities at his own expense; otherwise he is a paid civil servant, which nowadays he may be as well, but he should never let himself be that alone.

Beyond this, a gentleman is also generous, not only with his family and friends, but also with others. A gentleman of means should be generous in supporting financially those endeavors that he cannot personally undertake himself. If he can, he should contribute generously to good causes, though he should also be cautious about inadvertently contributing to bad ones. In principle, he should support churches, educational endowments, and arts establishments such as libraries, museums, musical foundations, public gardens, and the like — and above all, he should help the poor. In all these matters, however, he should exercise discernment.

A traditional role of the gentleman, in the days before welfare programs, was the relief of the poor and less fortunate, especially those who fell under his own charge as a landowner, often carried out as part of his role as a leader in the church. Gentlemen looked after the tenants on their estates, provided hospitality and even entertainment, and established charitable foundations for the impoverished, often operated by their wives. Urbanization removed some opportunity for this, and many gentlemen allowed their charity to the poor to be replaced by state welfare, which also meant that their wives were replaced by professional social workers. This was a major blunder because those social workers were often feminists, who, in good bureaucratic fashion, quickly discovered that they could create more business for themselves — their business being poverty and the social ills connected with it — by following their natural inclination, which was to throw all the income providers (i.e., men) out of their families. This ensured that the poor stayed poor and dependent on them, while also creating more poor to keep the whole enterprise going into succeeding generations. They started by making sure that only women could receive assistance and only those women who refused or severed marital ties with the fathers of their children. More recently they have extended their benevolence (yes, I know, a gentleman is not sarcastic) to the middle and upper classes as well, all with help from the divorce courts, which were established about the same time as the welfare system and which now quite happily throw even affluent men out of their homes.

By the way, all this is a major reason why there are no longer many gentlemen left today, because the boys are being raised by single mothers, and they never learn from their fathers how to be gentlemen; instead, they become gang members and criminals, and rather than shooting grouse and pheasants, they shoot one another. Remember these consequences when you are tempted to stinginess toward the poor.

All this has complicated the question of charity by distorting what we understand by "the poor." The poor should always be foremost in our minds, but deciding precisely which poor can be helped and how to help them presents problems. The traditional distinction between the "deserving poor" and the "undeserving poor," now widely ridiculed, may have carried more wisdom than we care to admit. Those labeled "the poor" are often single mothers, who are told that they are entitled to have children without fathers and to be supported at everyone else's expense. Mothers who have truly been abandoned by irresponsible men are suitable candidates for charity and always have been. But nowadays, most single mothers have not been abandoned, and feminist-inclined ones defiantly proclaim themselves to be single "by choice." They do not want charity. They want power, which means a share of your taxes—or, if they are your children, child support.

The result is that there is now much chicanery perpetrated in the name of charitable giving. Foremost are groups tugging on our heartstrings in the name of children—the same children whose poverty rationalized the creation of the welfare system. Whatever the charitable cause, the shrewd fundraiser will advertise it as being "for the children." But this can be more cynical than charitable. It is the job of parents to provide for their children, and you should never give to organizations that undermine other people's families or parental discipline or rights to their children.

Likewise, causes for "women and children" such as "battered women's shelters" are really just feminist organizations that help women get advantage in divorce cases, and those for "abused children" are not much better.

The other way to pull on our heartstrings is to appeal in the name of "the homeless." But here, too, you should beware of the optical illusion and remember that some 85 percent of the homeless are men, and almost all of them — virtually to a man — were once prosperous and productive citizens who were plundered and ruined by the same divorce courts (ask them) that have turned their children into "the poor."

So, whether it is children or the homeless, most problems of poverty today are concocted, often by the same people who are requesting your money to relieve the problem and who will use it to create more of the very problem they claim to be solving. So you have no need to feel guilty for not giving it to them, but you should give elsewhere instead. Your money might do far more good at a shelter for men.

This should also help with the always vexed question of whether one should give to beggars. Able-bodied young men and single mothers, however pathetic they may look, are different from the truly helpless. Sober elderly men and women, on the other hand, especially veterans, may well have a legitimate claim.

Giving to political causes presents different dilemmas. Remember that a gentleman — like a citizen — is an amateur. He exercises his civic duties as his time allows, and the time he devotes to it represents a sacrifice (a good thing). If, rather than taking the time and trouble for his duties, he instead gives money to professional activists and lawyers to perform his civic duties for him, he is farming out his citizenship (a bad thing). Worse, by paying professionals, he is giving them, too, an incentive to create more of the problem they are supposed to be alleviating. This is why otherwise good causes become bad causes, because they become dominated by miniature versions of what that great Russian leader (or troublemaker) Lenin called "professional revolutionaries." Whether it is environmental pollution, civil liberties, or whatever your pet project, if you want it done right . . .

3

EDUCATION

A gentleman is well educated, but unless called upon, he never shows it. Some European *savants* traditionally had few inhibitions about leveraging their learning to set themselves up as a privileged caste. "Gentlemen, never deny yourselves to be scholars," urged an Italian advice book from the Renaissance, "never be ashamed to show your learning, confess it, profess it, embrace it, honour it: for it is it which honours you, it is only it which makes you men, it is only it which makes you gentlemen."[62] Still, Anglo-Saxon[63] gents have preferred to be a little more reserved about the matter. "If ... you would avoid the accusation of pedantry on one hand, or the suspicion of ignorance on the other, abstain from learned

---

[62] Stefano Guazzo, *The Civile Conversation*, quoted in Pocock, *Doctrine*, loc. 1996 (chap. 7, n. 16), Kindle.

[63] The term "Anglo-Saxon" traditionally distinguishes anglophones from continentals and is not intended to suggest racial difference. During the British Empire, a racial distinction was indeed conveyed by the term "gentleman of color." Though taken to be condescending and eventually discarded, it has recently made an ironic comeback, as "people of color," at the instigation of the politically correct. So today a "gentleman" can be recognized as such without any racial qualifier, though the rest of the "people" apparently cannot.

ostentation," warned Lord Chesterfield. "Wear your learning, like your watch, in a private pocket: and do not pull it out, and strike it, merely to show that you have one."[64]

Like the rest of the gentlemanly code, education is more than just a finishing school or a claim to superior status (let alone — horror of horrors! — anything so vulgar as a means of acquiring a higher level of paid employment). Its importance is consistent with our theme so far: it provides practical benefits that are necessary for citizenship and leadership.[65]

You may think that this is a daunting topic, but the first and basic principle is this: *Do not be intimidated.* Yes, education requires time and effort, and ideally it should have begun when you were very young, but life is seldom ideal. It is true that we try to educate children early, and this is why the English aristocracy — along with its later imitators among the middle class, and in America, Australia, and elsewhere — shipped their sons off to boarding school at a tender age so that they would get a head start, not to mention the right accent, connections, and so on. (And no doubt you can imagine that they had other, even less

---

[64] *Works of Lord Chesterfield*, 177.

[65] As a modern scholar observes: "It was not from a passion for learning for its own sake; not from a wish to dignify outward life and leisure; not from a national instinct for a great past; not from a desire to reform doctrine or ceremony in religion; but first and foremost to meet a demand for better governance, to call into play, from new sources as well as old, forces better equipped for the more complex tasks of the modern state; it was for such an end, practical, and, in a certain sense, limited, that the Englishmen first grasped the weapons which the Renaissance held out to them from Italy." W. H. Woodward, "Studies in Education during the Age of the Renaissance," quoted in Pocock, *Doctrine*, loc. 2119 (chap. 6, n. 31), Kindle.

admirable motives.) But never fear. If you think that you missed your opportunity and that your own education is inadequate, you are in good company — the company of almost all of us. Many who have grown up since the 1960s have been the casualties of "progressive education," meaning they did not teach us much. But the more educated a man is, the more aware he is of his own ignorance. If you are ashamed of yours, that is a good sign, because you can remedy it with less effort than you may think. That is what men naturally do when they feel inadequate physically; they go to the gym. A similar habit will help you overcome your mental and spiritual deficiencies as well.

Education today has been debased everywhere, even in those snooty boarding schools, which is another reason not to feel inadequate. Even where it is still good, it is far from certain how much of it the boys ever absorb. The one lesson they always do manage to internalize very effectively is how to make others feel inferior. The genius of English "public school" education — like that of fancy institutions such as Oxford and Cambridge and the Ivy League — was not that it created an elite of the privileged, as its critics charge. The real value was quite the opposite: it created a standard that was then imitated right down the food chain to the "lower" orders, many of whom actually learned the material, motivated by the knowledge that they could improve their status, while the rich toffs in the public schools dissipated their days and their family's wealth devising sadistic tortures for one another. (Read *Tom Brown's School Days*.) Ironically then, it created an unparalleled system of *popular* education. Years ago, when I was a graduate student, an electrician visited my London garret to repair the sockets. Though he had obviously never graced the door of a university in his life (in those days, well under 10 percent of English youth attended higher education), when he saw the books of history on my desk, he made me ashamed by how much he knew on the subject of my specialized research. Now that Britain has followed America and France in adopting the peculiar snobbery that anyone without a university degree is a compromised human being, few B.A.s or even Ph.D.s will know as much about their nation's past as my electrician.

In fact, nowhere today is education so debased as in the universities and colleges, to the point where many people seriously question whether it is even worth spending three to six years and six figures attending one. Having taught in a variety of them for thirty-plus years, I can assure you, it most certainly is not, unless you concentrate in the physical sciences. If students (and taxpayers) knew how badly they were being swindled by the academies, even the most prestigious, the entire house of cards would collapse. So ironically, we may be returning to the days when few gentlemen even bothered to attend universities. They were originally created for priests and lawyers anyway, and those gentlemen who did go seldom stayed long enough to obtain a diploma.

If you are still young enough to be contemplating a college education, and you decide to fork out the necessary time and money, please at least consider a few things. First, few institutions nowadays offer the kind of classical education I describe below. A few still do, and at others you can find the necessary courses, so do take advantage of it. But beware: many are taught by instructors who are the same products of progressive education and have very superficial educations themselves, even at institutions that are always going on about their "rigor" and "excellence."

Most universities and colleges have now succumbed to the fashion of creating pretend degrees in make-believe disciplines such as Journalism and Environmental Studies. It must be said that this is partly under pressure from students like you, who are led to pursue these pretentious subjects under the illusion that it will procure them jobs that will make them rich and influential. In fact, you are cheating yourself. If you see your education primarily as training for a job, you will be proceeding directly contrary to basic principles of a gentleman, and you may be pointlessly sacrificing your opportunity for a real education. All the great universities—and all the great civilizations—of the past operated under the contrary assumption: that the natural rulers of society are men who have been trained in the classical liberal arts, not in the nuts and bolts of a trade, which a reasonably intelligent man can readily acquire on the job. This includes even the most prestigious "professions" (a fancy word for trades) like law and business (medicine may be another matter).[66] The first task was to create—you guessed it—*gentlemen*: men of the right character and outlook, with rounded educations and the self-confidence to acquire more as needed. The ideal course of study for such a man was in some completely useless field, like Byzantine history or Syriac languages. The resulting product might have no practical knowledge of anything, but when called upon, he could sort out matters of which he was totally ignorant, like the water board, or the health service, or the railroads of India. He could readily manage these affairs because he would understand how to educate himself. But never would he dream

---

[66] Miss Manners (a.k.a. Judith Martin) somewhere objects to this word, "professionals," and complains justifiably that it implies that the rest of us are amateurs. As we have seen in the case of a gentleman, however, the nonprofessional status is perhaps something to be embraced. At the risk of deflating the new snobbery using the old, a thin line ultimately separates a "professional," after all, from a tradesman.

of anything so narrow and self-defeating as to pay good money for a university qualification in Water Board Administration or Railroad Science.

The British Empire was run by men with degrees in useless subjects. In fact, it was built in the first place by men with no degrees at all—swashbucklers and scoundrels, most of them, men like Robert Clive, whose parents exported him across the world and who thankfully could not even manage to kill himself successfully but somehow succeeded in acquiring most of India and came back so rich that he could buy a seat in Parliament. After that, the operation was taken over by administrators from Oxford and Cambridge whose knowledge of India consisted mostly of Sanskrit.

The American Empire, such as it is, was built and run by more practical men, but often self-educated and also lacking in college degrees. (Abraham Lincoln is a good example.) When it came to imperial administration, they, too, eventually yielded power to an elite class. The ideal of an administrative elite was preserved in America and other republics in that last bastion of aristocracy: the diplomatic corps, admission to which still is (more or less) based on competitive examination of a kind reminiscent of the Indian Civil Service or the Chinese Mandarins.

The point is, if you are going to mortgage your financial future for a "piece of paper," make sure it comes with a real education behind it, one that distinguishes you with enduring knowledge rather than snob value and political ideology, and not some ephemeral skills that you can just as well acquire on your own.

But the other point is that you can also acquire the real education without mortgaging your financial future, by following the basic principles outlined here. So once again, never let yourself feel inferior. Even if you slept through your classes in Homer or Shakespeare, or were smoking dope, or never had the classes in the first place—do not despair. You probably know more, and the Ivy League graduates less, than you think. In any case, the deficiencies can be easily remedied. It can even be fun.

Finally, as we go through the subjects, remember that an education is not just about acquiring knowledge but also the critical faculties you bring to bear on it and the uses to which you put it. At the same time, the imperative of "critical thinking" has become another of those clichés invoked by educational professionals who may not always be so adept at it themselves. Someone once distinguished between a critical mind and a critical spirit, a useful distinction that seems to be lost on many academically employed scholars today, with severe consequences. A critical mind examines the knowledge it acquires with discernment and even a degree of healthy skepticism. A critical spirit (a.k.a., a smart-ass) simply delights in finding fault. Critical thinking cannot become a substitute for actually learning something. Confucius supposedly said that, while learning without thinking is pointless, thinking without learning is dangerous.

The Essentials

The traditional classical education began with the *trivium*— grammar, logic, and rhetoric—which comprised more than these terms suggest today and were actually more useful than many people imagine. They really involved an analytical approach to learning as much as its substance. We have already seen that the basics of grammar and rhetoric are essential for communicating effectively in speech and writing. After all, your thoughtful, handwritten letter composed on elegant stationary will lose much of its charm if you misspell *stationery*, like I just did, or misuse the word *like*, as I just did. Worse, you will be deceived by charlatans if you cannot spot these and more obvious horrors.

The trivium was accompanied by the *quadrivium* of arithmetic, geometry, music, and astronomy, and basic math has an obvious corresponding utility. Now we can move on to the fun bits.

The principal method for acquiring an education is still reading. Nowadays recordings and videos can be helpful as supplements, especially if you treat them like university lectures and take notes. But reading still has one major advantage: you can underline the interesting bits. It is always helpful, therefore, to have your own copy of a work, or nowadays you can download the classics, which allows you to underline or highlight the passages that might be useful or important to you later, plus write comments in the margins. Some recommend keeping a journal, if you can depend on yourself to have the discipline, but in any case, underlining is a good first step. Without some notes to aid your memory, most of what you read will be lost. At some point, too, you may want to use what you read in your own writing, because reading and writing complement one another, and both become more effective when done together, which is impossible without a body of underlinings or notes for reference. Remember the famous adage of Francis Bacon: "Reading maketh a full man; conference a ready, and writing an exact man."

Learning to write well is also part of your education, and it helps you to process and apply what you have read, and therefore retain it better in your memory. But writing is more active and therefore more difficult than reading, especially at first. If you do it well, you will find it hard, and if you find it hard, you are probably on the right track. The renowned economist John Kenneth Galbraith (who also wrote novels that are, I have no doubt, better than his economics) said that anyone who says that writing is easy is either a terrible writer or a terrible liar. An effective and fairly effortless method of overcoming the impediments and acquiring the skill is to jot down short sketches or paragraphs in the margins of your books (electronic books make this easy) or in a notebook, giving your reactions to what you have just read. If you are motivated, these can be expanded and pieced together to form essays, articles, perhaps even books.[67]

LITERATURE

This is an important one, but it is easily acquired. All the names may seem intimidating at first, but there are really only three items that you must know right away:

- Greek and Roman mythology, plus the major Greek classics: Homer, the *Iliad* and the *Odyssey*; Sophocles, *Oedipus Rex*.
- The Bible, preferably the King James or Douay-Rheims versions, with all the *thees* and *thous*: You probably already know the stories of Adam and Eve, Noah, David and Goliath, Samson, and Daniel in the lion's den. Here are a few more of importance: the stories of Abraham, Moses, David, John the Baptist, Jesus' ministry, the apostles, and Paul's letters.

---

[67] Helpful suggestions on writing can be found in Charles Murray, *The Curmudgeon's Guide to Getting Ahead: Dos and Don'ts of Right Behavior, Tough Thinking, Clear Writing, and Living a Good Life* (New York: Crown, 2014), chaps. 14–18, "On Thinking and Writing Well."

• Shakespeare: He wrote about thirty-seven plays, but not all are essential to know. Roughly:

Tragedies
>   *Hamlet*
>   *Macbeth*
>   *Julius Caesar*
>   *King Lear*
>   *Othello*
>   *Romeo and Juliet*
>   *Antony and Cleopatra*
>   *Troilus and Cressida*

Comedies
>   *A Midsummer Night's Dream*
>   *All's Well That Ends Well*
>   *As You Like It*
>   *The Comedy of Errors*
>   *Measure for Measure*
>   *The Merchant of Venice*
>   *The Merry Wives of Windsor*
>   *Much Ado about Nothing*
>   *The Taming of the Shrew*
>   *The Tempest*
>   *Twelfth Night*
>   *The Winter's Tale*

Histories
>   *Richard III*
>   *Richard II*
>   *Henry V*

There you have it. That is all you need to know to consider yourself—and be considered by others—to be an educated man.

Perhaps you think that even this minimal list is daunting. Nonsense. Each one requires only a few evenings' reading to acquire the basics. Start with some summaries, so that you know the plots and characters. These are easily accessible on the Internet or in books. From there, move on to excerpts, so that you know the most famous stories and passages. Here again, you can find these on the Internet and in any bookstore. You can also find summaries and dramatizations of these works, either shortened or complete, on Internet videos. Once you have this grounding, you will realize that it is not so difficult as you thought, and you might well be moved to read longer passages or even the works in their entirety.

So, that is all there is to an education? Of course not, but this provides you with the foundation, on which the rest is built. So, when you see allusions to these works in later ones, you will recognize the source. And remember: no matter how much education you acquire, a gentleman never displays his learning gratuitously. In the short run, your immediate aim is to avoid humiliation if someone mentions these things and you have no notion of what they are talking about. In fact, nowadays, most people have no notion about most of these things, but you will not realize that until you know them yourself, and you must protect yourself against the smarty pants who will try to corner you. Needless to say, you do not then turn around and become the smarty pants yourself. Once you have this covered, you are safe, and no one will know otherwise, so you can relax and start to enjoy the rest at your leisure.

Because once you acquire this knowledge, I am confident, you will want to acquire more, for these things are inherently interesting and they expand your mind, outlook, and spirit, much as workouts in the gym expand your muscles and the things you can do with them. In both cases, you will also find that your self-confidence increases. At some point, you will begin to realize that you are becoming one of those people who previously made you feel intimidated. (But, being a gentleman, you will not now use it to intimidate others.) At some stage, you may well become shocked by the ignorance, shallowness, and arrogance of those whose education consists mostly of degrees from pretentious schools.

Once you have acquired this foundation, you will probably have become aware of what other items you should know but do not. To go further, lists of the fifty or one hundred greatest books of all time can be found on the Internet, but since these may not be reliable, you could start with *The Thousand Good Books* of John Senior. Here, too, no one reads them all, so from this point on, you can pick and choose what appeals, and if you dip into, say, *Madame Bovary*, *War and Peace*, or *The Grapes of Wrath*, without finishing it, at least you have something to say on the topic. Now whatever you read you will be able to read more effectively with your knowledge of the three foundational items mentioned above.

Incidentally, if you want to read some books on the ideals, realities, and shortcomings of past gentlemen, you can start with the novels of William Thackeray, Anthony Trollope, Jane Austen, and Charles Dickens.

HISTORY

This takes more time, but most people enjoy reading about history, so make sure that your reading has some purpose and focus. Otherwise you will get sidetracked into entertaining diversions at the cost of the essential foundations. Here, too, you can find summaries of large periods of time or countries or events on the Internet, either to read or to watch on video. These will give you the broad picture before you get into the details. Start with Western history, especially the high points:

- Greece and Rome
- the Renaissance, Reformation, and Enlightenment
- voyages of discovery, the creation of empires, and their decline
- the big revolutions in England, America, France, and Russia
- the Napoleonic wars and the American Civil War
- the two World Wars

If this seems like a lot, remember that no one knows it all, and your aim is not to know it all. Your aim is to acquire the basics. Once you have this grounding, you can go back and read more details about both the West and the rest of the world. Then you can also read or watch the entertaining stories, biographies, historical novels, docudramas, and the rest, and they will mean far more to you.

PHILOSOPHY

For many, philosophy is the most intimidating, and much of it can be tedious indeed. But again, do not despair. No one reads it all, and some philosophers are unreadable anyway, so it is enough to know why you should know about them and their significance and a few famous passages without actually reading them in their entirety. If, as is likely, you discover some specific reason that you want to explore some specific theme or philosopher in detail, then of course you can do so, but you cannot really know what this might be until you understand the big picture. Here, too, start with summaries and excerpts so you get the grand sweep and the few essential details. This will also allow you to find out which philosophers you might want to read in more detail, or which ones you should look at when you need to. But to start, you should know at least a little about the following:

- Socrates
- Plato
- Aristotle
- Cicero
- Augustine of Hippo
- Thomas Aquinas
- Niccolò Machiavelli
- Martin Luther
- John Calvin
- Thomas Hobbes
- John Locke
- René Descartes
- Jean-Jacques Rousseau
- Thomas Jefferson
- G. W. F. Hegel
- Karl Marx

It is worth emphasizing—emphatically—that you do not read these books because they are necessarily correct or morally good. And do not expect to agree with all of them; if you do, you need to think again. In fact, some may be positively evil, and concerning others the consensus of educated opinion is divided. You read and familiarize yourself with these books because, for better or worse, they have been the most influential according to the test of time. It is even possible for a book to be on the list—most notably, Marx's *Capital*—because of its enormous influence, even though it is also thoroughly unreadable, manifestly erroneous in its prophecies, and morally pernicious in its effects. If we wish to remove it, we must first weaken its influence, which, like it or not, requires some knowledge of it. But the point, again, is do not struggle through it all, but be aware of what is in it.

As for the important categories of philosophy, we have already seen that knowledge of formal logic, and the ability to detect logical fallacies, is inseparable from grammar and rhetoric and can be highly useful for argumentative gentlemen. Ethics is another branch of philosophy that has obvious applicability for gentlemen who are not skillful at wiggling out of their moral dilemmas. For many people, political philosophy is the most engaging and the most likely to come up in discussions, especially public ones. Most of the names above wrote important political philosophy—again, for better or worse. Economic theory also came straight out of philosophy. From Augustine onward, philosophy and political thought become inseparable from theology, so it is good to be conversant in the basics at least of that.

Music

Most people like music in one form or another, so learning the elements of musical knowledge can be enjoyable. The fundamentals are not difficult: musical notation, the Western musical scale, major versus minor keys, the basics of harmony. And of course, you can readily listen to it all on the Internet. You should also know the major historical eras of musical development and the major composers who exemplify them:

• Medieval (plainsong or Gregorian chant)
• Renaissance

- Baroque (Bach, Vivaldi, Handel)
- Classical (Mozart, Haydn)
- Romantic (Beethoven, Brahms, Schubert, Chopin)
- Modern (Stravinsky, Schoenberg)
- plus major composers of opera (Verdi, Puccini, Rossini) and ballet (Tchaikovsky, Prokofiev)

ART AND ARCHITECTURE

Nowadays learning about art and architecture is easy because familiarity with the visual arts can readily be acquired from the Internet or books. Yet nothing stimulates your interest like a trip to an art gallery, if there is one locally, or when you travel. Also, do not neglect architecture, which can be appreciated simply when you are walking down the street or, again, if you travel to a new city. Architecture, including landscape architecture, is especially important because it determines the environment in which we all live our daily lives and is not an experience limited to special excursions to a gallery or museum. If you wish to be poncy, or just prepared against others who are, you can learn the meaning of peculiar terms such as *painterly*. Otherwise, just know the general periods of art history. Some roughly parallel those of music, so you can learn them together:

- Ancient
- Medieval
- Renaissance
- Baroque
- Rococo
- Neoclassical
- Romantic
- Realist

As you get into Modern and Contemporary art, you will find a huge assortment of strange schools. Only a few are likely to come up in conversation, and the rest no one really understands or can be expected to. These are enough:
  * Impressionism
  * Pointillism
  * Dada
  * Art Nouveau
  * Cubism
  * Surrealism
  * Socialist Realism

SCIENCE AND MATHEMATICS

Gentlemen who are well educated in other respects are often deficient when it comes to science and mathematics. Yet others who lack extensive educations in the arts and humanities may be knowledgeable in the sciences. This is because many men naturally gravitate toward technology and its background, at least insofar as they find it useful in their daily or professional lives. The public schools in most Western countries can still (generally) be relied upon to provide quality teaching in these fields, with a minimum of fashionable trends or political ideology, and the governments that fund those schools know that, on these topics, they do not have the luxury of adulterating the curriculum with political silliness if they want to have anything worth governing.

It is good to have at least some knowledge of the basics of the following:
  * mathematics, including geometry and algebra
  * physics, including astronomy
  * chemistry

- biology
- geology (at least a smattering)

Even if you are not well versed in science itself, a knowledge of the major figures in the history of science rounds off any claim to a classical education: Aristotle, Ptolemy, Copernicus, Galileo, Kepler, Newton, Darwin, and Einstein.

Beyond this I cannot help you, because in these fields my own education was deficient, so you can strike out on your own or wait for the next edition of this book.

FOREIGN LANGUAGES

A truly educated man speaks at least one modern foreign language and knows at least a little of the ancient ones, notably Latin. Language learning can be time-consuming, but again, there is no need to despair. When you are reading about Greek and Roman mythology and history, take the opportunity to learn a few essential words in Greek and especially Latin. Even a smattering can enrich your experience. The poet Ben Jonson once accused a rival of knowing "small Latin and less Greek," but the rival was Shakespeare, so that may have been enough. No one but the experts just picks up Homer and starts reading it in Greek anyway, so knowledge of a few key words or phrases gives you far more than most people have and enriches your reading of literature, history, philosophy, theology, political thought, and the like.

As for modern languages, an educated man knows at least one world language in addition to his own. During and after the Renaissance, this was Italian, but the Italians failed to extend their influence by building a modern empire, so troubling to acquire the language of Dante and Boccaccio, for all its glories, is now limited mostly to art historians, opera afficionados, and migrant

Albanian fruit pickers. Italian was replaced by French as that became the language of culture, literature, philosophy, diplomacy, and even science and the military. Later, German came to rival French in some areas, and these are probably still the two most important languages to know, at least a little. Nowadays, ambitious young people are keen to learn Spanish, Russian, Mandarin Chinese, Arabic, Farci, and other languages that are spoken in large regions of the world that they believe will help their careers. But other than Spanish and Portuguese, these are difficult and time-consuming for Westerners to learn, so while it never hurts to acquire some basics of a foreign language, any extensive study may best be saved until you are sure that you will really need them.

Of course, modern languages are especially helpful for traveling and living abroad, which is why you should learn them *before* you set off on your foreign adventures, but that is also an excellent way to perfect them, as we shall now see.

The Grand Tour

Starting around the eighteenth century, a young gentleman was expected to round off his classical education by touring the cultural centers of Europe. "According to the law of custom, and perhaps of reason, foreign travel completes the education of an English gentleman," wrote the historian Edward Gibbon, though he did not sound completely convinced of it himself.

This is much easier today than in the past, though, by the same measure, it is in danger of defeating its own purpose. Affluent young people today already put a premium on travel, and the current fashion of the "gap year" has some affinity with the earlier practice. The usual time was after the university, but that was when aspiring gentlemen started the university in their teens, and most never stayed long enough to obtain a degree, because they were wealthy enough not to need one, so I am not advising you to drop out of college in order to travel around the world. As always, the travelers have attached a certain social snob value to recounting and comparing their latest adventures. Like most snobbery, that attached to exotic travel is actually vulgar, and you have my permission to regard it as such, though not to practice reverse snobbery.

Anyone who has ever cringed in embarrassment at hearing the loud, whiny, or nasal accent of one's compatriots in a foreign setting knows that international travel is no longer a mark of accomplishment or refinement. The stereotypical figure, once known as "the ugly American," nowadays has equally crass equivalents among the British, Europeans, and others.

Fortunately, it is still possible to both distinguish and improve oneself through travel, though, as always, it requires some thought and preparation. Random travel is pointless, so choose your destinations with a purpose. The most profitable method is to visit places that you know through your education—or the education that your travel plans can inspire you to acquire. The traditional sites were selected to complement the classical education: the ruins of ancient Greece and Rome, the Holy Lands, Renaissance Italy, or cultural sites in France and later Germany and Austria, plus—for Americans and other colonials—England. Today's more exotic destinations (from a Western perspective) simply require more preparation, but it is still profitable not only to learn about the history and culture but also to understand why you should know it in the first place.

Spend some time reading before you go. A good guidebook, like a Blue Guide, is indispensable, but do not stop there. Knowing *why* you want to visit a specific place rather than another one gives your adventure some purpose and contributes to your improvement as a gentleman. This makes it more likely that you will retain what you learn and grow from it in mind and spirit, rather than just trying to absorb random and insignificant facts with which to bore your friends and family.

Here, too, a little time invested in learning the language can make a huge difference, and foreign travel naturally provides an effective opportunity and inspiration. It is now much easier than in the past, with online courses and translation applications for telephones. Yes, with English now the world's *lingua franca*, you can get by and be adequately understood in most capital cities and major tourist attractions. But you also limit yourself and your experience, and it will show. Nothing is more tedious to the natives or demeaning to yourself, when you walk into a shop, than to have the first words out of your mouth, in English, "Do you speak English?" You will be marked and treated like part of the horde. If nothing else, learn to say, in the most courteous form of the local language, "Pourriez-vous m'excuser si je parle anglais?" ("Do you mind if I speak English?") It is true that this courtesy may be lost on the French, Russians, and others who believe that they speak a world language and that it is your responsibility to speak to them in their own tongue and on their own terms rather than the reverse. More accurately, it is mostly the Parisians and Muscovites who harbor this supercilious attitude, to the point of refusing to speak English even when they can, but outside the major cities you will find less English spoken anyway, so the point is the same.

And by the way, the tempting shortcut of relying on translation devices, uncorrected by some minimal appreciation for the nuances of the local language, will prove of limited utility and could result in some embarrassment. We are told that even so august a corporate notable as the Pepsi-Cola company found that its popular advertising slogan, "Come alive with the Pepsi

Generation!" was rendered rather less successfully into Chinese as promising that "Pepsi brings your relatives back from the dead." And if the American Dairy Association really was so naïve as to assume that its own cutesy slogan, "Got Milk?" could survive a literal electronic translation intact, it learned otherwise when the question, intended to remind shoppers during excursions to the supermarket, was instead received by Spanish speakers as a query about their lactation.

Here is where knowledge of world or regional languages such as French, German, Spanish, Russian, or Chinese can prove useful because it connects you to educated people of all lands. But knowing a little of even a minor language can be helpful and satisfying. In the provinces and in countries that are not accustomed to hearing foreigners speak their language at all, even a smattering will immediately make you stand out, if not a celebrity. The locals will be impressed and flattered that you have made the effort, even if you can utter no more than rudimentary phrases, and they will treat you like a visiting dignitary. This can also bring practical benefits when it comes to finding a meal, a bed for the night, a public washroom, and so on.

It is a cliché that foreign travel also broadens your horizons and provides new perspectives on the world. As an instructor in comparative political systems, I cannot help but take satisfaction that a major justification (or excuse) for the Grand Tour was originally, in the words of Catherine Macaulay, to "distinguish the different natures of different governments, their advantages, their disadvantages."[68]

---

[68] Quoted in Michelle Cohen, "'Manners' Make the Man: Politeness, Chivalry, and the Construction of Masculinity, 1750–1830," *Journal of British Studies* 44 (April 2005): 312–329, 323.

Yet dangers do lurk here. You should, of course, begin your adventure with an open mind and treat foreign ways and customs with respect. No one is resented more than the loud foreigner who complains at length and every opportunity about whatever does not conform to his experiences or voices constant opinions about the superiority of his own country. Understanding foreign customs with patience and forbearance can be fascinating and can indeed open perspectives even on your own country that you may have never considered. The best book ever written on American politics, after all, was by a French visitor, Alexis de Tocqueville.

Yet, for the educated young man nowadays, an opposite danger may be greater. Be wary of allowing yourself to be seduced by the novelty of your host country. Not every foreign custom is "charming," and peculiarities that you may initially regard as "quaint" may turn out to be bothersome. Even worse, some believe, may be the effect it can have on you. "By going abroad the youth may be polished out of his rusticity," wrote Richard Hurd in his *Dialogues on the Uses of Foreign Travel* (1764), "but may easily wear himself into the contrary defect, an effeminate and unmanly foppery."[69] The traditional English or American gentleman was expected to be conversant in Italian architecture, French cuisine and wine, and so forth, but he was never to forget that he was not Italian or French—about whom, in private, he might well complain at tedious length. Above all, he was not to fall into what was called "French politeness," which was regarded,

---

[69] *Dialogues on the Uses of Foreign Travel Considered as a Part of an English Gentleman's Education: Between Lord Shaftesbury and Mr. Locke* (Cambridge: W. Thurlbourn and J. Woodyer, 1764), 105, 160, quoted in Cohen, "Manners," 322.

in Hurd's term, as unmanly. Many were said to return from the Tour "who knew no toils but those of the toilet."

Even Macaulay's rationale of an education in civics could be self-defeating, with serious consequences, she herself warned, when the youth "grow charmed with everything that is foreign, are caught with the gaudy tinsel of a superb court, the frolic levity of unsuspecting slaves, and thus deceived by appearances, are rivetted in a taste for servitude." Another British authority did not like the political influence of Europe one bit, though his reasons seem somewhat contradictory, first being disturbed "that so many should return confirmed republicans," yet meanwhile "so many others, captivated by the charms and outward appearances of the courts abroad, should entertain too favourable notions of monarchy."[70] Since you are reading this in English, I will point out that the English-speaking countries in particular have long feared the degenerating moral effects of continental Europe and sought to distinguish themselves and keep a healthy distance from the infection, conveniently assisted by the English Channel, the Atlantic Ocean, and even larger bodies of water. I will only suggest that this may not have been entirely irrational chauvinism, and leave it at that. But whatever your national

---

[70] He was relieved to observe that "their religion indeed will be in no great danger of being changed, as there is not much temptation to it [in Europe], but as they carried but little abroad with them, there is a great hazard of their losing that little, and returning without any." Thomas Sheridan, *British Education 1756*, rev. ed. (London: 1756; repr., Yorkshire, England: Scolar Press, 1971), 29–30, quoted in Lisa Mangiafico, "Aspects in Creating a Gentleman: Education and the Grand Tour in Eighteenth-Century England" (master's thesis, University of Massachusetts, 1992), 42, https://scholarworks.umass.edu/theses/1762.

origins, remember your roots and be proud of your own country, while not being blind to its defects.

On returning home from foreign travel, it is not necessary to irritate your provincial friends and relations by advertising your exploits abroad, let alone by sporting a beret or lederhosen. You may also be wise to refrain from attempting to entertain them with the mechanical Jew that still seems to be on sale at some tourist attractions in Eastern Europe. If others raise the topic and ask, you are now in a position to speak from experience.

Religious Faith

You may not see this as part of your education, but most certainly it is. The consequences of neglecting it could be severe. We have already stipulated that an educated man is familiar with the basics of the Bible and the works of major philosophers, many of whom were Christian or of other faiths. But there is more that is essential.

It has been said that "a gentleman believes in God because by and large he is confident that God believes in him."[71] This irony is not so flippant as it might sound. Religious beliefs — at least the best ones — impel us to obey the rules not simply because otherwise bad consequences will ensue, including serious punishments to ourselves. At some point, we at least try to obey because gradually we come to feel that to do so is to act in ways that are consistent with the logic of the universe. There is no better preparation for being a gentleman.

For, as stated earlier, being a gentleman is not just a matter of obeying rules. It involves internalizing the rules so that they become part of your personality. This is not easy to achieve,

[71] Sutherland, *English Gentleman Is Dead*, 13.

unless it was part of your upbringing from the earliest age, and even then it is hardly reliable. For the rest of us, a lifetime is required, and this internalization is precisely the aim of religious faith as well and something it accomplishes more effectively than any secular belief system or code of conduct. You do not simply strive to obey the rules; you begin to feel abnormal when you act contrary to them, and you feel more natural and comfortable when you act according to the rules than when you transgress them. At a certain age, and as this process becomes successful, you also start to become seriously annoyed with others when they do not obey the rules, but this, too, must be kept under control.

There is no need for me to preach about it. The great German sociologist of religion Max Weber, who coined the term "Protestant work ethic," observed that Christianity aims to bring man's "actions under constant self-control." Weber himself noticed how directly this purpose, even when promoted by some of the more strident religious zealots, corresponded to the ideals of the gentleman:

> This active self-control, which formed ... the cool reserve of its adherents ... can be seen [in] that respect for quiet self-control which still distinguishes the best type of English or American gentleman to-day.... The Puritan, like every rational type of asceticism, tried to enable a man to maintain and act upon his constant motives, especially those which it taught him itself, against the emotions.... The end of this asceticism was to be able to lead an alert, intelligent life: the most urgent task the destruction of spontaneous, impulsive enjoyment, the most important means was to bring order into the conduct of its adherents.[72]

[72] "Calvinism," pt. A in "The Religious Foundations of Worldly Asceticism," chap. 4 in *The Protestant Ethic and the Spirit of*

Over the centuries, Puritan preachers and other churchmen struggled to convince gentlemen that they should redefine their status (or "honor") by more elevated standards than was their proclivity. Most aristocrats and would-be aristocrats were naturally inclined to measure their worth by their secular status: their birth and ancestry, their titles of honor, wealth, lands and estates, offices and professions, accomplishments, fame and reputation, military prowess, sexual conquests, their hawks and hounds. The Puritans taught them that all of this was vain and pointless unless they also learned to behave themselves ethically and according to a well-informed conscience. Naturally, the churchmen frequently failed in this enterprise and, by their own admission, were often ignored. But in the long run, they succeeded more than you might think, and the reason was this: religious faith actually made life easier and more secure, because it made the competition for status less backbiting and cutthroat. All the other accoutrements of gentle status could readily be lost, and a man could be deprived of his honor and fall into disgrace. But religious faith could provide a status that would endure the ups and downs of one's fortunes, especially the more this was recognized. It would also put him on the moral high ground, above the rivalries, the petty bickering, and the relentless pursuit of status.

Nowadays, when men as a group have fallen to about the lowest status in their history, it might be worth considering the value of taking the moral high ground and rising above the sordid pursuit of individual "empowerment," the finger-pointing, and victim-mongering, and seek a code of conduct that is more elevated than that of others.

Capitalism, rev. ed. (New York: Charles Scribner's Sons, 1958; repr., New York: Dover, 2012).

I cannot enter here into all the instances of where the faith of all the world religions contribute, in varying degrees, to gentlemanly behavior, but consider just one: we discussed earlier that a gentleman must not be afraid of being hated, and one of the gentlemanly qualities that is most difficult to put into practice is how to respond to reproaches, insults, criticism, and hatred. You might recall that the seminal figure of the religion that shaped the ideal of a modern gentleman — Jesus — provided precisely such a model of how to respond, not with vitriol, bitterness, and reciprocal anger (though he did know when it was appropriate to overturn a few tables), but with humility and sacrifice. Remember that when you are tempted to think that religion is just some namby-pamby exercise in moralizing and nagging, or that being a gentleman is simply a matter of wearing tweeds or a bowler hat.

Keeping in mind your task of having to rule the world, remember, too, that every great empire and world system of administration has operated according to some elevated religious or quasi-religious ethic. This served to instill a sense of duty and pride in the civil servants and keep them honest, efficient, and dedicated: for the Romans this was Stoicism; for the Persians Zoroastrianism; for the Chinese Confucianism; the Holy Roman Empire had Catholicism; and the European maritime empires had their various versions of Christianity. Even the Soviet Empire tried to use Communism for the same purpose.

When the ruling ethic deteriorates, and before the empire collapses altogether, the administration degenerates into an oppressive bureaucratic tyranny, with the functionaries expanding their turf and making business for themselves by creating the problems they are supposed to be solving. This is precisely why today's welfare states have become a nightmare for men like you. The Christian ethic that at one time governed charity and voluntary social work has disappeared and been replaced mostly by feminist ideology, so the functionaries now prey on the families they were ostensibly created to serve: separating men and women, confiscating children, criminalizing adolescents, plundering and incarcerating fathers, and shaking down taxpayers. So again, do not think that these principles do not have consequences for you.

This is not the place to prescribe a complete curriculum in theology. Just remember: it has occupied the best minds from all civilizations throughout history. A gentleman does not dismiss or sneer at religion, any more than he would ridicule history or science or art. An educated man does not ignore, much less does he denigrate, the things he does not understand. It is not necessary that you know everything; only that you show respect to those who know more and try to learn from them.

If nothing else, you will be wise nowadays to remember one major and universal principle of religion and consider carefully its implications: in every culture, religious faith provides the principal basis for regulating sexuality, relations between the sexes, and marital and family life, which we will consider next. Not all religions do this in the same way or equally effectively, but they all do it. It is no accident that the status of men has deteriorated directly alongside the status of religion. In societies where religion is still respected, men are still respected. So, if you think that these matters do not concern you as a man, then you are not paying attention. Here, too, it is not necessary that you agree, but you must at least understand what is going on.

4

WOMEN AND FAMILY LIFE

Relations with women are inevitably at the heart of manhood. It is no accident that all the classical advice books emphasize the central importance of how a man should relate to women. And it is also no accident that today's modern advice books that are helpful on other topics become inadequate when faced with this one.[73]

Women are the foil against which a gentleman defines himself. This means that today's dominant culture trends strike at the heart of what it means to be a gentleman and why we must now not so much redefine the word as recapture its essence and defend its basic features. Sexual (or "gender") relations are not simply the occasion for today's crisis of manhood. They are the result, in part, of recent generations of men having neglected precisely the matters addressed by this book.

---

[73] I have recommended McKay's *Art of Manliness*, which offers useful instructions on the different options for tying a tie, landing an airplane, and other everyday necessities. But chapter 4, on relations with women, is much less helpful, for he, too, has succumbed to the new sensibilities, probably as the price of publication by an established publishing house.

A GENTLEMAN'S GUIDE

Being a gentleman always means comporting yourself according to high standards, but you must also be discriminating (to use an unfashionable word) about which standards you adopt. You are not required to conform to every fad that Hollywood or television or the National Organization for Women decide are desirable redefinitions of the "new" masculinity—or one of an ever-expanding assortment of redefinable "masculinities." A large part of a gentleman's dilemma today is to discern this difference. As always, you are required to show appropriate deference and respect to women and to sacrifice your own comfort and safety for theirs. You are not required to wear high heels or pretend you are pregnant.

Even more seriously, today's sexual-political agenda is not only disorienting for everyone; it is a formula for open-ended expansion of the government's power. The claims of feminists and others who want to politicize the relations between men and women that they are "oppressed" (by *you*, never forget) rationalizes ever-increasing power for politicians, judges, lawyers, and functionaries. This power is for use against men like you. If you think you can appease it with the kind of weasel words that are now the daily fare from men in public life ("I have always had the greatest respect for women," blah, blah), then you are not a man but a weasel. You must withstand this temptation. Men serving as heads of families are the principal rival to, and check on, government power. While they have traditionally had allies—community leaders, clergymen, teachers, journalists, university dons—these former watchdogs have mostly become lapdogs. Most have deserted their posts and run away—either that or they are too busy enjoying the perquisites they have acquired with government money to even think about biting the hand that feeds them. That leaves you, because you cannot be bought off even if you want to be. Although it might support women and mothers, no welfare system will pay you to be a man and a father, and no judge or social worker will take up your cause and defend you against a female or any other "oppressor." You are the end of the road, and the buck stops with you. It is you who must build our institutions all over again, from scratch.

It is critical to understand that today's "gender war" was declared by the ideologues: feminists and other radicals, lawyers, government functionaries and their hangers-on, facilitated by media pundits, craven politicians, and weak men generally. It is decidedly not a war between men and women. This is more than a perfunctory, politically correct piety. For when it becomes a war between men and women, men lose.

Indeed, a cardinal principle of a gentleman is that he does not compete against a woman — or at least he avoids it whenever possible. First, it is undignified and inherently emasculating. But following from this, when men and women compete with one another, the competition is always one-sided, and men always lose. A particular man may appear to prevail in any particular contest. But morally, the man always loses. For only two outcomes are possible: First, the woman is victorious, which is taken to prove that women are equal to or superior to men in every way, that there is nothing distinctive or special about men, that the competition entitles the woman to exult in her triumph and gloat over her victory and rub his nose in his defeat and humiliate him for his weakness. Alternatively, the man is victorious, which proves nothing, except perhaps that men enjoy using their strength to dominate and oppress women, and there is no point in exulting or gloating, which he is not permitted to do even against another man, let alone a woman. Men should never compete against women, and they must refuse to do so whenever possible. This is already the natural inclination of most men, who desert institutions (which they are now spontaneously abandoning in large numbers) such as universities, schools, workplaces, clubs, sporting competitions, and even the military when they become dominated by women, precisely because they understand instinctively that they cannot compete effectively and that the competition itself is inherently degrading. The relations between the sexes must be ones of complementarity, not competition. The moment the sexual dynamic becomes competitive, standards of fair play become impossible, the sexes are set at warfare with one another, and important social institutions such as families disappear.

As always, women as a group are sacrosanct. Both civilization and women themselves demand that women be treated with respect. If they are not, we will hear about it from women, men, and everyone. "He who speaks badly of women is a boor," says one authority from the Middle Ages.[74] This is a given and cannot be avoided or changed, even if you want to, which you should not. No matter how unjust the current cultural and political regime of the social justice warriors, women themselves are inviolable. This principle, too, has not changed and never will. Women as a class are sacred and always will be.

But this does not mean that individual women have carte blanche; nor that you must grovel when faced with either a woman's favor or her disfavor. Women have rules to obey as well. A gentleman honors the rules and enforces them, first on himself, then on those close to him, and finally on others, insofar as he is able, including the women in his life who misbehave.

You must also understand from the start that women are different from us in fundamental ways. For purposes of peace and

---

[74] Gillingham, "From *Civilitas* to Civility," 271.

politics, you may have to mouth the occasional cliché about how "gender" differences are "socially constructed," but you must never allow yourself to believe your own piffle. If you do, you could well be jolted back to reality with a summons to court or a pair of handcuffs.

It is often observed that women want contradictory things. But it is important to understand why. It is not some irrational peculiarity in the female brain but results quite logically from the somewhat tragic situation in which women are placed if they are not rescued from it by men like you. And it could well become the tragic flaw of our civilization if men like you do not understand and respond a bit more forcefully.

The problem stems from perhaps the most relevant difference between the sexes for your needs today, which lies in our respective ways of pursuing power. Human beings inevitably crave power. Political philosophy has long recognized this—Machiavelli, Hobbes, and Nietzsche being the most obvious examples—and a major aim of both political philosophy and practical politics has been to control the power drive specifically of men.

Women also crave power, but, unlike men, their craving can be pursued in two broad ways. They can achieve power through their relationship with a man, or they can achieve it on their own. To a point, these two avenues can be pursued together as opportunity permits, obvious examples being Lady Macbeth and Hillary Clinton. But sooner or later, if unchecked, this duality will create serious conflicts both for the woman and for the society (not to mention for the man). On the one hand, women want strong, powerful, and masculine men. On the other hand, they are not immune from craving power purely for themselves, which ultimately must come into conflict with that of their naturally more powerful men. Thus, they are willing to emasculate the very men whose power they admire and desire, whereupon they will then despise the men for their weakness.

This is why not all women can be given everything that some of them claim to want—especially those who most crave power. This is also why women admire men who stand up to them. It is not enough for tough guys to stand up to bad guys. The tough guys we truly admire also stood up to women when they were demanding silly things. (See Humphrey Bogart in *The Big Sleep* or *To Have and Have Not.*) These are the tough guys we lack today, and this is the tough guy you must be.

This paradox has been exploited by both feminists and governments, and it is what modern men have been too weak to withstand. It is why advice books like this one lose no opportunity to inculcate all kinds of useful manly virtues and skills, from changing a tire to wrestling a grizzly bear, and then turn around, like craven sissies, and mouth high-minded but contemptible lamentations about the horrors of "sexism." We will try to avoid this servility, and so must you.

Next, understand that women need to be protected. For women, it is of overriding importance that they not only are safe but that they feel safe. They do not like risk, and they feel no stigma about expressing fear. You may encounter silly women who express a thrill at reckless behavior, but when things go wrong, it is you who will be blamed. That is why you must make the decisions. The inescapable fact is that women not only need to be, but demand to be, protected. They do not expect to protect themselves; they expect to be protected by others. If they do not feel protected *by* you, they will demand to be protected *from* you. No third option is possible, and they can and will find any number of champions either among other men or (more likely today) among the state officialdom to make sure that they are, and that means the penal apparatus: police, courts, and jails. And this is precisely why we now see the proliferation of new and flexible methods available to expropriate, remove, and incarcerate you: "sexual harassment," "domestic violence," "date rape," "sexual assault," and the all-purpose "abuse." Too many men bought into the foolish notion that they did not need to protect women. Women *will* be protected, one way or another, and they will be protected by men. The only question is whether it will be by you or the gendarmerie.

Likewise, women need to be provided for. Again, you must guard yourself against believing the party line. (Mouthing it is one thing; swallowing it quite another.) They may claim that they do not need a man to provide for them, and they may well command a salary equal or superior to yours. They may even enjoy paying the restaurant bill. But all this has nothing to do with a desire to provide for themselves or for you, which they will not do. It is another assertion of independence and power, and that means independence from you and power over you. Once you are married or even cohabiting, she can quit her job at will, but you will remain responsible for paying off the mortgage and the car loan. She can leave the marriage at any time, and you could pay, in addition to mortgage and car, spousal support. Once she is pregnant, the same woman who previously asserted her independence will have no hesitation about demanding a monthly government-coerced child support check from you many times in excess of what is necessary to raise a child, with no requirement to prove that the money is for a child, and free of any reciprocal obligations to you, living a life of leisure as a kept woman on your salary.

I do not say these things out of a desire to be "sexist" (a meaningless word). I say them because you must have no illusions if you wish to live like a man. You must accept the responsibility to protect and provide for any woman. It is therefore critical to choose a woman who acknowledges this and accepts the traditional rules and division of labor, rather than one who wants to assert her "equality" (another meaningless word in the relations between the sexes) and "independence." The bottom line: avoid such women.

Courtship

The term "courtship" itself sounds archaic. This is because true courtship long ago degenerated into dating, which, in turn, gave way to hooking up, and from there to cultural and legal warfare between the sexes. Each stage in the process entailed a shift in power away from families to individuals, from parents to children, from the mature to the young, from the wise to the foolish, and from all of us to the functionaries and gendarmes of the state.

THE PROBLEM

True courtship involved rules that were controlled by families, meaning mostly parents, with assistance from the other relatives, the church, and the community. These rules recognized both the importance of regulation to the well-being of the entire family and community and the dangers to everyone of leaving romance and sexuality to the control of young people, and therefore out of control.

With dating, control shifted to the couple themselves, but, of course, it was the man who was expected to take the initiative. This placed an awesome responsibility on young men that most were not prepared to fulfill. The result was anxiety and fear. Many became either pathetically awkward or unpleasantly forward or some unpredictable combination of the two. The first made the man miserable, and the second made the woman miserable, and neither provided the groundwork for a lasting romance.

As the rules disintegrated altogether, this logically gave way to "free love" (i.e., sex) and then to hooking up. Revealingly, this is generally rationalized by the career obsessions of (or pressure on) young women, which leaves them "no time" for leisurely romance but still plenty of time for sex. As usual, many young men, finding themselves with a bonanza of easy sex, raised no objection. Feminism led the women to believe they could enjoy uncommitted, purely physical sex, as men seemed to do, and that this would "empower" them with the strength of men. Since, for most women, this was obviously not the case, they then learned—also under feminist tutelage—to avenge their inevitable hurt feelings using accusations of new pseudo-crimes such as "date rape" and "sexual assault," even when everyone knew full well that it was consensual. This had the added benefit of "empowering" the wronged women in ways they never expected. The men, young and foolish enough to think that all that free sex really was free, paid for their folly by finding themselves hauled before pseudo-courts in universities or even real courts and charged with peculiar-sounding crimes that they did not understand and against which they could not defend themselves. By abandoning the accepted rules in favor of our own urges, we have gone, as one attorney says, "from courtship to courtroom."[75]

In short, we now find ourselves embroiled in precisely the chaos our grandparents predicted when we abandoned the time-tested rules and insisted that we could handle it better ourselves.

[75] Jed H. Abraham, *From Courtship to Courtroom* (New York: Bloch, 1999).

In the meantime, all this progressive freedom and equality leaves men like you in need of some order being imposed on all this (other than being scolded by the sanctimonious of both the left and right), in order to avoid making a fool of yourself, find a good woman, and stay out of court and jail.

THE SOLUTION

First, you should realize that courtship can be enjoyable and exciting rather than intimidating. Following a few simple rules—nowadays mostly self-imposed—can help make it so.

First comes the question of what constitutes a good woman. The traditional distinction that all societies make between good women and bad women is now politically incorrect. But if you want to demonstrate your broad-mindedness and progressivity, you may pay for it with the loss of everything you have, including any children, with years of poverty, and possibly with prison followed by permanent homelessness. Bad women have many weapons nowadays, deadly weapons designed for use specifically against none other than you. The stakes are high.

In general, a good woman is one who accepts the virtues of modesty and chastity and who wants to be courted. A woman who expresses her determination to demand her "rights" and "equality" and who wants to take the initiative is trouble. She may assure you that she sees her "oppression" coming not from you but from "society," with its outdated norms and arbitrary conventions. She may even tell you that you are oppressed by society as well, with all the intolerable burdens it places on men to be masculine. But she cannot take out her hurts on society, punish society, or have society hauled up on charges of sex crimes. The lawyers will not issue summonses to society, and the police cannot put the handcuffs on society. These recourses are available only against individuals—like you.

The scenario of a quick hook-up followed by a criminal accusation is certainly "empowering" for bad women. A bad woman wants to be "empowered." A good woman wants to be courted.

But a good woman—from here on, we will refer to her by her proper title of "lady"—is far from mindless or passive. On the contrary, she has high standards and knows the right rules, and she will enforce them if you are too weak to do so. A bad woman has a hundred off-the-cuff opinions, which she loses no opportunity to express but which she can also quickly change when it suits her convenience. In fact, this is a good way to spot one. (You might check the bumper of her car.) A lady, by contrast, has not opinions but fixed principles, beliefs, and convictions. She may be quiet about them most of the time, but, when tested, she will stick to them, even against you. She will also use them to inform you when you are about to make a fool of yourself, because this is an important role of a lady. But she will not judge you for it because she will know that we all make fools of ourselves.

Because she has principles, a lady will also have strong defenses. These must be respected. Breaching her defenses should not be seen as a problem. On the contrary, it is the challenge and the joy of courtship. How you go about it will determine your subsequent relationship and allow you either to grow in affection or decide to move on to someone else.

Next is the question of where to find a lady. American and other English-speaking women today—and increasingly, women from other Western countries—often do not fit the above description. In fact, they have a worldwide reputation for being loud, overweight, and opinionated. Above all, they are highly prone to litigation, such as harassment and rape accusations and divorce, which brings still more accusations, like domestic violence. Sensible men avoid them. To find good women, white men are looking to Eastern Europe, and black men to Brazil and Africa, and all men to the Far East. To counter this (and prove my point), the ideologues have devised yet another weapon in their arsenal of criminal-sounding accusations: the suggestion that men who pass over liberated western women for more agreeable women in more traditional societies are guilty of "sex tourism," but, so far, there is not much they can do about it.

If you live in an urban environment with many young singles or in a university community, most of the women may not appear to be ladies. But this is not true. There are many ladies out there, even if they live in less fashionable neighborhoods, attend less snooty colleges, or have less prestigious jobs. It is also possible that displays of feminist bravada are youthful fancies out of which an intelligent but poorly brought up woman can be encouraged to grow. Here you must use your discretion.

THE PURSUIT

OK, so you have your sights on a particular woman. What do you do now?

Yes, you are sticking your neck out, and you run the risk of failure and rejection. Taking risks is your lot as a man. You must accept it. Men who have no problem facing down the most formidable bully or criminal or battlefield foe can become simpering sissies when having to face a woman. But if she is a lady, she will respect you for taking the risk, and if not, then the matter is not worth your worry. Besides, she will be taking a risk, too, if she encourages you, and you must help put her at her ease.

Let us revert for just a moment to the time when courtship was controlled by parents. The custom of asking permission of the woman's father *before* beginning courtship will strike some as quaintly old-fashioned. But before you dismiss this, consider a few things. First, many people do still practice it, and believe it or not, it still has some merits. It makes the entire matter aboveboard from the start. Everyone knows the purpose, and there are no awkward pretenses to the contrary. It also signals to the woman herself that your intentions are serious. Moreover, there are advantages in getting to know her family, as well as their obvious advantage in getting to know you. A woman with a family that is solicitous of her marital and sexual welfare is more likely to be the kind of woman whom you should marry, the lady described above. And marriage is a union of not just two individuals but of two families. The wisdom of this is something you will appreciate when you have children. It will help you recognize a suitable match for your own daughter.

If none of this convinces you and you are still scoffing, you might consider the value of this knowledge: it might be to your advantage to know if her family are the kind of people who are going to gang up on you in a divorce proceeding.

Still, I am assuming that, for some, because you are reading this book, if nothing else, this first step is not an option and that you are largely on your own.

First, rid your mind of the notion that you are out to achieve something. Courtship is an art and a joy in itself, and the whole process should be enjoyable for both of you. If it does not work out, you can move on without embarrassment, and if it does, you can look back on it as the foundation of your relationship.

Another problem with changing the rules for male-female relations is that it subtly altered the purpose of the process by discarding marriage and substituting sex. Yes, love is still presumed to play a determining role, but without marriage as the final end, love itself becomes debased. The fastest way to rid the situation of awkwardness, therefore, is to remove from your mind this notion, inculcated in so much of popular culture today, that you must express your romantic interest through some physical contact, even something seemingly so innocuous as a first kiss or holding hands. There is no need to hurry any of that. It will happen spontaneously if it happens at all. Simply eliminating the possibility in your mind from the start will leave you feeling extremely free and spontaneous. Treat her like a delicate flower that cannot be touched. It is not expected, and it should not even be a possibility.

Yes, today, it seems like even some women expect some physical expression of affection on a first encounter and feel insulted if they do not get it. But this does not make it any less awkward and cheapens the value of holding hands or a kiss. You can find better ways of letting her know of your continued interest. In fact, the more reticent *you* are about that, the more easily you can move forward in more important ways.

Once you have eliminated this burden, you can freely acknowledge that your interest is romantic. If you are strongly attached to one another, this creates an electric atmosphere of extended flirtation and expectation. If this does not happen, then it is perhaps best to move on. If it does, you should draw this out and advance the relationship slowly. You will never have precisely this opportunity and this moment again, and it is your chance to build a relationship that is solid and joyful.

Such is the state of accepted practice that many guidebooks for men now available on this topic crudely intermingle romance indistinguishably with sex. The few written according to traditional religious tenets may have forgotten the wisdom behind their own principles, but at least they put you on safer ground, even if you are not a religious believer. As always, I will offer just a few gratuitous suggestions of specific interest to today's aspiring gentleman:

Err on the side of formality. We are so overly familiar nowadays that everyone is immediately on a first-name basis. This creates a kind of reverse familiarity that is artificial and false, but ironically, it does allow you to convey respect to her by adopting a more formal approach. If your circumstances permit it, try addressing her at first as Miss Smith. Do this for a while, and at some point, you could ask permission to address her by her first name. You can do this, too, with an air of irony. This makes it an important moment and will achieve a real familiarity that is not artificial. Then linger over her name, as if using it is a privilege. And by the way, if all this annoys her, as it may, that may be a quick way to find out that she is not for you.

Make known your romantic interest, but indirectly, with irony and humor and self-deprecation. "I must admit that I do have a weakness for . . ." and then describe her: ". . . tall thin Armenian women with red hair. If you happen to know any . . ."

Conduct some of your courtship in writing. E-mail is helpful, but for unexpected impact also use letters (you know, on paper, nice paper) or the occasional card. It allows you to say precisely what you want, with nuance, subtlety, elegance, irony, enigma, and sometimes ambiguity. The very fact that you are writing shows your interest, so you do not have to be direct or forward. It also shows that you are willing to make an effort for her. It is therefore a nonthreatening way to advance the relationship. Do not tell her your feelings, at least not right away and not explicitly.

A GENTLEMAN'S GUIDE

Discuss subjects of mutual interest, but, at some point, get around to the question of love. Do it abstractly at first, without mentioning her. And please, *never, ever* say, "I love you," or anything remotely like it. If you are young and the two of you seem to "hit it off," you may quickly feel emotional infatuation. *Do not mistake this for real love or let it go to your head.* You, as the man, must keep a cool head, since excessive emotional attachment at first can lead you into trouble. Instead, tell her your philosophy of love and your understanding of what it means, and ask hers. She will get the message.

LOVE

Speaking of which, let us linger over this subject for just a moment. Modern Western society has a debased notion of love. It is largely emotional, and we equate love even with the superficial infatuation. A more elevated understanding will certainly help with courtship. First, it is no accident that the roles of men and women in courtship are different. Not only can feminism not change this, but it has no real desire to. The man's role is more active and the woman's more passive. This is more than a matter of who initiates the matter and takes the lead and pays the restaurant bill. A woman's overriding need is to be loved. She will respond to true love and overlook a thousand flaws and mistakes if she believes she is truly loved. For a man, being loved by a good woman is a great joy, but an excessive need to be loved is considered unmanly and for good reason. Again, men have responsibilities that must often take precedence over being loved and, as we have seen, may well require your willingness to be unpopular and even hated. You must accept this. This is why we insisted previously that what men do need is to be respected.

Without respect you will lack the authority to take the some-times unpopular measures that are necessary to be a responsible husband, father, citizen, and ruler.

Many people, especially young women but also some young men, have an emotional approach to love. But yours should be more elevated. Expressing love in terms of emotion is usually awkward for a man, so there is no need to force the matter. Deeds speak louder: not only flowers and dinner but little courtesies and subtle (very subtle) compliments. As a man, you express love not by *saying* but by *doing*. That conveys to her that among the things you will do is protect and provide for her, along with any children, and stay with her regardless of the difficulties.

Above all, love requires sacrifice from both men and women, but yours may have to be greater. You are the one who must prove your love to her, not the reverse. The only way to really value love and reliably measure it is by what it costs. Words can be nice but also empty because they are cheap. Deeds prove your love, as lovers from time immemorial have recognized. This is why words such as "I love you" must be used sparingly and should probably be saved for the marriage proposal. If you truly love her, after all, and if your love means anything of substance, you should be willing to make a lifetime commitment. Otherwise, there is something (like your freedom) that you love more. Euripides said that "he is no lover who does not love forever."

Notice I have said little about "compatibility." I have said something, and I will say more, about you both having a healthy attitude toward marriage itself. But I have said almost nothing about whether you and she have similar interests, like to do things together, have an emotional attachment to one another, or even share the same values. Sharing the same values is important, but they must be the right values. I minimize compatibility partly because I am confident that you will attend to it without being told, but also because I think it is overrated. Initial infatuations never endure, and even substantial shared interests can change. For most of human history, these criteria never entered into it, and nothing suggests that the marriages were any less happy. On the contrary, substantial evidence suggests that they were more so; they certainly endured much better and not simply because people could not "get out of" them.

Some of the most famously loving marriages in history have been arranged for family or political reasons. In traditional and peasant societies today, they are still effectively arranged. And while I am not advocating this, it is worth noticing that these marriages succeed because people understand and observe ac-cepted rules, the most important of which is that marriage is indeed for life. When they fail in the rules, they have family, friends, churches, and communities to "encourage" (or force) them to express their contrition and try harder. I have already suggested that emotions are not a reliable indication of real love, which must be created by experience and sacrifice. It was when people started "marrying for love" that they started divorcing at whim. This, too, is a product of our debased understanding of love. And here, too, it is your job as a man to uphold a more elevated understanding of love. Both these changes, marrying for love and divorcing at whim, were brought in under the name of women's liberation — though, as usual, immature and hedonistic men were often willing accomplices — and you can be sure that it is the liberated women who will howl the loudest about this paragraph.[76]

---

[76] For a different view, see Murray, *Curmudgeon's Guide*, chaps. 32–33.

THE FOLLOW-THROUGH

Courtship should never end. Once you marry, continue the process. Treat every occasion with your wife as if it were your first date, with words, flowers, meals together. Continue to approach her as something delicate. Above all, anything physical should be approached gradually—and sparingly. And do not overindulge in sex, even after marriage. Treat it sparingly, as something special. Speaking of which ...

Sex

Given that you are reading this book, and therefore not likely to have been raised according to the traditional rules, this may involve the most difficult reorientation of your thinking. This is where you—and I mean your entire generation—may have to show the greatest change and strength of mind. But the rewards will be great. You cannot shirk this.

It is hardly news to say that men are obsessed with sex, especially young men. This is precisely why young men should not be permitted to rule the world without serious guidance and preparation. Every stable and prosperous society insists that men must get their sex drive under control before they can claim leadership, but young men who are raised to do this at an early age have a big advantage. Getting control in other ways is also important. Needless to say, immoderate alcohol and drugs and other indulgences are also not conducive to self-control, and they make you quite the opposite of a gentleman. But in some ways, sex is the big one.

A little history and some current politics may impress on you how high are the stakes and what you have to lose or gain. Controlling your sex drive is more than a matter of heeding the scoldings of your maiden aunt. Sexual self-control lies at the foundation of every successful civilization.

The obvious and outstanding example in our own political culture is, once again, the Puritans, who created America, modern Britain, and effectively all the modern English-speaking societies—that is to say, the most successful societies in history. As we have seen, they also laid the foundations for the creation of the archetypal gentleman. The Puritans were the first—and in many ways the real—founding fathers of what became the United States, and they continued to exert a dominating influence on the generation of the American Revolution and well beyond. Meanwhile, in England, they also created the world's first revolution and effective representative government, thus laying the foundation for the British empire and the political culture of the other English-speaking nations. The Puritans were breathtakingly important.

Their very name is synonymous with self-control through ascetic morality, including (but not limited to) matters of sex. The poet John Milton wrote of Oliver Cromwell, "Commander first over himself; victor over himself, he had learned to achieve over himself the most effective triumph." The Puritans made self-control through moral discipline the basis of an ethic of public service that created history's most successful, stable, prosperous, and free societies. Virtues like diligence, frugality, punctuality, sobriety, duty, obedience, and, yes, chastity were what put the Anglophone nations at the forefront of modern history, which they have dominated ever since.

More recent counterexamples may make the point more vividly and show the dangers of not doing it right—especially recent cheap and dangerous imitations.[77] The most obvious is Islamism,

---

[77] Even atheistic regimes such as the Communists, who tried to codify sexual license, found they were not exempt from this rule

the radical form of Islam, which is also obsessed with sex. This deadly ideology seeks to impose a superficially similar but far more extreme puritanism with much less successful results, creating societies of instability, stagnation, and of course terror. And yet their superior level of self-control may be putting Western society at their mercy. Not only getting sex under control but *how* we get it under control is vitally important.

Since the rise of the Playboy culture in the 1950s and 1960s, many men seem to feel entitled to have as much sex as they can get, and some have managed to get plenty. (It was this cultural change, incidentally, that debased the concept of a "gentleman's club" from a place to which men retreated for a brief respite *from* women to a place to which they repaired to express lewdness *toward* women.) This is foolish, and we are now paying the price, as shown clearly in the recent epidemic of accusations of sex (or "gender") crimes: "sexual harassment," "sexual abuse," "sexual assault," sexual this and sexual that. By their sexual self-indulgence, men today have put a weapon in the hands of their enemies to enslave themselves. ("O God, that men should put an enemy in their mouths to steal away their brains!" Shakespeare was speaking of alcohol, but the gonads can betray you equally well.) In this sense at least, it may truly be said that men have brought their troubles upon themselves.

When sex becomes the dominant currency in a society, then that society becomes dominated by people who can control the

---

and had to reimpose order. "The Revolution ... cannot tolerate orgiastic conditions," Lenin thundered: "Dissoluteness in sexual life is ... a phenomenon of decay.... Self-control, self-discipline is not slavery, not even in love." Clara Zetkin, "Reminiscences of Lenin" (1934); Marxists' Internet Archive, 2012, https://www.marxists.org/archive/zetkin/1924/reminiscences-of-lenin.htm.

market in sex and effectively use it as a tool and a weapon to increase their power. This is not heterosexual men, who have nothing to gain and everything to lose. It is women, especially politically radicalized women, and, more recently, militant homosexuals and transgenderists who will get the upper hand, many of whom do not like men like you.

Conventional wisdom today believes differently, that it is men who benefit from sexual promiscuity. But conventional wisdom is seldom wise.

It is true that every society practices a double standard. Men are permitted and sometimes even encouraged to be more sexually promiscuous than women. Some women complain that it is unfair, but there are logical reasons for it. Social stability demands the sexual discipline of women more than that of men. We can see the reasons today all too plainly, as single-mother homes are exploding and, with them, the welfare rolls and bankrupted governments and taxpayers. Armchair moralizers quickly blame this on male irresponsibility. Male irresponsibility plays a part, but a small part. The decisive factor is female irresponsibility. The reason, as the late Shakespeare scholar Daniel Amneus pointed out, is not because men are better but because of simple biology. If 95 percent of the males are chaste, the remaining 5 percent can sire as many bastards as the entire 100 percent together, if the women are willing. If 95 percent of the females are chaste, the problem is under control.

Recognizing all this, however, does not absolve men of their culpability for our present troubles; far from it. First of all, men (again, young men) since about the 1950s have not only indulged sexually themselves; they have also encouraged female promiscuity, for obvious reasons. This was a fatal mistake.

Hugh Hefner, founder of *Playboy* magazine, saw the early feminists as allies because they, too, were celebrating free, uninhibited sex. He assumed their motives were as simple and crude as his own. He was lusting after women. But the feminists were not lusting after men; they were lusting after power. Later, he was shocked and perplexed when they turned against him and denounced him as an oppressor of women. But this was predictable. Like other hedonists, he was a fool and walked straight into a trap. But I must say, many of us in the 1960s and 1970s were similarly foolish.

By encouraging both male and female promiscuity, men handed control over the terms of sexuality to women, and, of course, it was the worst women who availed themselves of the new power. Though many people think that women are naturally in charge of the realm of sex, children, and the family, this is never true in stable societies. They were always kept under control by older women and older men. The reasons have now become painfully clear: the natural weapons of power-seeking women are two: sex and children. Today, the sexual rules are dictated and constantly changed by young, highly politicized women. They do this not so that they can have more sex but so that they can have more power, which they acquire by using sex as a weapon against men. This is the clear trajectory of feminist politics: offer easy sex, and then criminalize male sexuality by calling it "sexual harassment," "sexual assault," "rape," "trafficking," and so forth. And it does not stop there, because you can criminalize even the responsible men and fathers through divorce.

All that free sex that men (some men) enjoyed in the 1960s, 1970s, and 1980s, was a massive honeytrap, even if no one consciously planned it that way. We were lured into the trap by the temptresses of sexual pleasure. Now the trap has been sprung, and we are paying the price with accusations of quasi-crimes that criminalize us as men and by divorce proceedings that confiscate our children and criminalize us as fathers.

A GENTLEMAN'S GUIDE

Coming from the generations that allowed this mess to happen, I can only urge you to learn from our mistakes and not perpetuate them. Your task is to undo the mess. If you wish to resume your role as the natural leader of society, you must get this chaos under control. It will not be easy, and you must start with yourself.

PROMISCUITY (YOURS)

It is also true that advice books like this one traditionally winked at male promiscuity. But we cannot wink at it any longer, for now we can see the consequences, such as a trip to court or to jail. The proof of this is that some men are already spontaneously withdrawing from marriage and even from female companionship altogether in the Men Going Their Own Way (MGTOW) movement. Some seem to think that if they do not marry or have children, they can continue to have sex for recreation without consequences. This is foolish, for the feminist-dominated gendarmes have more ways than ever to punish you, and they are devising new methods all the time. So it would seem that circumstances have now made this a good time to make up for the excesses of the past and show a little caution. Others go so far as to boycott not only marriage but sex too, so at least they are more consistent. It is ironic that this new impromptu celibacy, born of necessity, seems consistent with some traditional religious practices and perhaps testifies inadvertently to their wisdom. If men are going to foreswear sex, they may as well do so out of principle rather than out of fear. After all, fear opens you to contempt and ridicule—thus today's complaints about male "fear of commitment," "puerility," and similar clichés—whereas principle gives you authority.

In fact, the entire MGTOW complaint illustrates the triumph of bad women, who have been allowed to ascend to unchallenged heights of power because of the past self-indulgence of bad men. You should understand this as definitive proof that recreational, extramarital sex, so far from "not hurting anyone," has serious consequences. If you are going to toy with the affections of women and use them for easy sex—no, you are not a criminal; no, you are not a rapist; no, you do not deserve prison or even eviction from the university; and nothing can possibly excuse false accusations or a legal system so crooked that it rewards them. But you are a cad, and you are playing with fire. Never forget the old line about how "Hell hath no fury …" If I may wax theological about it for just a moment—and you can add this to the list of practical benefits from religion—a false rape accusation may be a hideous miscarriage of justice from man, but it is a perfectly valid reminder from God of a higher law that, as a gentleman, you are expected to observe.

So by all means, join the MGTOW men and abstain from sex with my blessing, but while you are at it, at least direct your boycott at a constructive purpose: to marginalize bad women, encourage good women, and possibly even—despite your professed intentions—find one of the latter to marry.

PROMISCUITY (HERS)

Having established sexual control over yourself (like Cromwell), you now have the authority to encourage it in others. This does not mean that you perch yourself atop a public soapbox and start threatening passersby with hellfire and damnation. The place to begin is with the women you choose and how you treat them.

This is not just cheap quasi-feminist piety; quite the opposite. For it means not only that you must refrain from indulgence with promiscuous women; it also means that you must grasp the nettle and insist on chastity from any woman with whom you associate and certainly from any you intend to marry. This is your duty not only to yourself but to other men and also to good women and true ladies. If you think this is some "old-fashioned" prejudice on my part and that you are being broad-minded by dating or marrying a woman who is promiscuous, you are asking for trouble. There are sound reasons why men have traditionally demanded chastity and even virginity from women they plan to marry. You ignore this at your peril.

First, there is no reason that she must remain faithful, because the terms of divorce today are such that she will not be penalized for adultery or for deserting her marriage. On the contrary, she will be rewarded, and it is you who will be punished for her adultery or desertion. Second, you will have no guarantee that any children produced will be yours. Here again, she will not be punished. You will. You could well end up paying 50 to 75 percent of your salary for eighteen years (or more) of child support for children who are not even yours.

But today's extreme circumstances reveal a deeper and more universal principle: a promiscuous woman cheapens the currency of sex. This is why, contrary to feminist victimization dogma, the main enforcers of the sexual double standard are women, and a promiscuous woman is far more likely to be labeled a "slut" and ostracized by other women than by men. She makes it more difficult for other women to use their sexuality as leverage to get good men (i.e., gentlemen), which is what sensible women do. A promiscuous woman is willing to exploit her sexual allure as a tool and a weapon, perhaps because it makes her feel attractive or loved or simply powerful. But in any case, the promiscuity is only the beginning. She has more methods for weaponizing sex nowadays than ever before, and they include accusing you of crimes and quasi-crimes against which you cannot defend yourself.

Of special note here is the problem presented by divorced women and single mothers. Marrying a widow is a time-honored tradition in many cultures, and some even make it an imperative on the families of the deceased (the Old Testament, for example). It not only provides the children with a father but also relieves the society of having to provide for the family.

Today's phenomenon of mass divorce and single motherhood is a different matter altogether and has precisely the opposite effect. Marrying a divorced woman and especially a single mother is one of the most dangerous things you can do. Yes, it is possible that she was truly abandoned by her husband through no fault of her own, as the media like to report. Not only are there women to whom this does happen; some are treated by the divorce system as inhumanely as are men. (Often their husbands had some professional connection with the divorce industry.) But such women usually do not have custody of their children. Statistically, in any case, it is far more likely that she is willfully depriving her children of their father from her own private grievance. If so, she will not hesitate to do the same to any children she has with you. At the very least, a woman who has broken her marital vows owes you a detailed explanation of the grounds upon which she did so, and you are well advised to insist upon hearing and verifying it before you take vows with her.

So, stop pretending you know better than thousands of years of history and every stable civilization and every credible religion. For your own sake, and for the sake of good men and women everywhere, be a good man, avoid bad women, and find a good one.

"Sexual Harassment" (etc.)

Yes, these nasty little subjects keep coming in and ruining a good moment. That is precisely what they are intended to do: poison romance between men and women. But this is a serious problem and must not be avoided, say the scolds in their self-fulfilling way. Yes, it is indeed a problem, because they have made it one.

"Sexual harassment," "sexual assault," "sexual misbehavior," "sexual misconduct," "sexual abuse"—no one really knows what these terms mean, and that is precisely the point of using them. They are intended to be vague, and they are constantly being redefined (even "rape"), so that whatever you do (like writing an advice book for men) can be made to fall into one of these categories if an aggrieved woman or an ambitious prosecutrix wants to bring a legal case against you.

It is therefore essential that you cut through the jargon and the posturing and understand these matters clearly. The only way to avoid falling afoul of these accusations is to avoid the practices—and the people—that occasion them.

Most people still think that sexual harassment refers to men in positions of superior authority using their leverage to extort sexual favors from female underlings. This is what you are supposed to think, because if you think that is all it is, and you know that you would never do such things, it will be easier to snare you. Needless to say, such is the behavior not of a gentleman but of a cad and bounder. And not surprisingly, such behavior has been prohibited by professional and legal codes since long before the feminists used the accusations to leverage political power.

But if you think this is all there is to it, then you think that it is the concern only of cads and not of you, in which case you are either a fool or simply an average man.

Today this term refers to *any* romantic overtures from any man whom a woman considers beneath her. As posters on the Washington Metro and elsewhere declare quite clearly, if the woman welcomes the advances, then miraculously they are not harassment. It is her subjective state of mind, not your objective deed, that determines if you are a criminal. In short, this a tool to criminalize male behavior, and that means you.

The best way to avoid harassment accusations is to avoid feminist-inclined women. Do not pursue them, and do not associate with them. The first time a woman starts dropping lines about "gender equality," let her know that you regard that as a direct threat to you. The next time drop her.

At the risk of really revealing "retro" behavior, you might consider the wisdom in adopting the old rule of politely refusing to speak to any woman to whom you have not been properly introduced. There are ways to meet good women. Talking to strangers is generally unwise, at least in the Western world and especially in urban settings, where good women do exist, but they are likely to be camouflaged by a sea of wannabe prosecutrices.

Appearance and Attire (Again)

All the advice books (especially recently) excoriate men for looking at other women than their own, and rightly so. Do not do it. Every man naturally wants to, and for men who spend large parts of their adulthood single, as many do nowadays, it can become an unthinking habit that is difficult to break. You must consciously train yourself not to, even when you are alone.

Needless to say, even a single gentleman looks at women with discretion. Staring and ogling are not acceptable, much less comments, catcalls, and whistles. These acts are ungentlemanly in themselves, even aside from the ammunition they provide to feminist complaints about male puerility. Yes, it is mostly working-class men who thus indulge, and it is quite obvious that many working-class women enjoy the compliment and respond to it. But the more subtle you can render your flirtations, the more they will be perceived as gentlemanly. Here again, nowadays they can be taken as actionable offenses (even "visual harassment") and even semi-criminal ones ("visual assault," "visual rape"). However silly this has become, some of it, at least, is easily rectified because it was always against the rules in the first place.

The feminists' politicized jargon and its legal implications are not necessary. It is not the behavior of a well-brought-up gentleman. A gentleman does not comment on the attractiveness of women except in the proper romantic context. The quaint old habit of introducing a gentleman "and his lovely wife" probably always annoyed some women, and very likely their husbands. As it was never really correct in the first place, on this score I am willing to concede that it is unnecessary. If nothing else, you are binding yourself henceforth to acknowledge every other couple present in the same terms, and woe to you if you slip up.

The main role of men when it comes to a woman's clothing and appearance is to tell her that she looks nice. When it comes to your own woman, do it — profusely, especially when she really does, because it requires effort. The fact that you are not comfortable going into details should tell you something. Never do it. Let her attend to the details.

By the same measure, women have standards to observe as well in order to show respect to you and others, and if she does not observe those standards, she is insulting you and others around her. A lady understands this or at least is willing to understand it, and that should be an important consideration for you in choosing one. Here, too, you do not need to concern yourself with any details. Your only concern is to decide if she has crossed the line of respectability in her appearance. If she expresses an intention to accompany you in public looking like a prostitute and displaying herself sexually to the world and the gaze of other men (which some foolish men seem to encourage, as if their woman is some kind of trophy), that is a major insult to you, and you are well within your rights—indeed, it is your duty—to say no. No details, no explanations. It is not your role to instruct her on how to dress. She may dress as she likes. And the corollary is that you may publicly accompany whom you like. You simply indicate that she has crossed the line and you will not be seen with her in public until she presents herself respectably. End of discussion.

This carries over into your family. Once she is your wife, the matter becomes even more important. Putting herself on display for other men to observe sexually is the equivalent of you allowing your eyes to wander, and some women today seem to think that this is their entitlement. If you have any doubt, wait to hear the howls these paragraphs will elicit from feminists, even though I am saying, shorn of their jargon, what they say: that a woman should not be a "sex object." Yet for you or me to say it strikes directly at their self-appointed role as the arbiters of "gender" relations and therefore at their most coveted commodity, which is power.

In your other associations, you are likewise entirely within your rights to associate with whom you please. If you think that a woman, any woman, is dressed in a sexually provocative or disrespectful matter—for example, in a business setting or a church—you may politely decline her company and conversation or keep it to a cold minimum. There is no need to say why. You might also suggest that your own wife or lady friend do likewise.

After all, you may be avoiding temptation (even mental temptation), and she may well respect that. This was traditionally the role of mature women, some of whom would now willingly resume it. But it starts with you.

If your company or school or university has a dress code, you should likewise have the leadership to see that it is enforced. Many are afraid to do so nowadays, for fear of some kind of accusation. Supporting your employer is another indication of courage today.

"You are asking a lot," I hear you say. "Expressing disapproval of how someone else dresses? Don't people have a right to dress as they like? What business is it of mine?" Yes, they do. But you have the right to associate with whom you please. In fact, you also have a right to say what you please in private conversation, but just because you have the right (at least presumably you still do), it does not mean you should always exercise it. It is not necessary to say anything; in fact, it is often better not to say anything. First, it can be construed as rude. Secondly, nowadays it might be construed as some kind of gender crime. But unless matters have become more extreme by the time you read this, you still have the right to walk away from anyone you choose. Summoning the moral courage may not be easy, but once again, moral courage is the corollary to physical courage and a major part of being a man.

When you become a father, this will be your natural role, and here again it is your duty: to supervise your daughters' (and sons') propriety, beginning with their appearance and dress and extending to their behavior with boys and men. This is a natural and indispensable role of fathers. If the feminists object, they are objecting to the very existence of fathers, which is precisely why they are constantly trying to get fathers removed from their families and put them in prison.

Marriage

Marriage at one time was a respected institution, and men who married were more respected than those who did not. It has also long been recognized that married men are happier, healthier, live longer, and earn more money than single men. Marriage gives you lifetime female companionship and someone to love and take responsibility for besides yourself. It unites two people in such a way that they have a permanent interest in the well-being of one another, plus other people and other things, as much as of themselves. It therefore integrates you into the civilization as a long-term stakeholder. Every successful civilization honors and protects this institution in some form.

Yet today, young men like you scoff at marriage, call it "just a piece of paper," and see no reason to formalize their family ties. Indeed, many are not even forming family ties. I am not going to wag my finger at you over this. But for your own sake and everyone else's, you must face this squarely and get it right.

Young men are left ignorant of marriage's importance because even today's self-described "advocates for marriage" do not always get it quite right. They preach platitudes because they are afraid to speak the truth for fear of being scolded by the gatekeepers of political orthodoxy. But you must cut through the pieties and understand the truth, because it could affect your future dramatically.

One cliché today, popular among the moralizers, is that marriage exists to control the promiscuity and other undesirable traits of men. Like most clichés, it contains an element of truth, however simplified. But marriage can civilize you only if you understand its purpose, which should inspire you to become one of its true and enthusiastic defenders, as opposed to another irritating moralist.

Traditionally, a married man was indeed expected to assume a code of decorum superior to that of a bachelor. The standard rule was that once a gentleman is married, his former associations are terminated unless he chooses to renew and continue them. Your old drinking companions and other embarrassments no longer have any claim on your attention, and you are not required to acknowledge the association unless you choose to do so. Marriage offers a chance to start over, and it is a good idea to take advantage of this. What was said before about any man being capable of being a gentleman, regardless of how humble his origins, is aided by marriage. Marriage helps you to not look back.

It is a common misconception that marriage is a concern for women rather than men. It is true that wedding preparations are a multimillion-dollar industry controlled almost entirely by women. But if the wedding industry is the domain of women, this is equally true of the divorce industry (to be discussed shortly). In other words, you have strong practical interest in the integrity of marriage in general as well as your own marriage in particular. Leaving marriage matters to the sole control of women is foolish. The bad women among them will change and manipulate the rules to control men like you, and that is precisely what they have done. If nothing else, it is best to have your family involved in the preparations as well as hers.

It was traditionally accepted that marriage legitimizes sex. Outside marriage it is "fornication" or, if at least one party is married, "adultery." Inside marriage, sex is consistent with the principle of chastity. There are logical reasons for these prohibitions, but most people no longer understand them. You must.

As a young man, you may think that all these easy women are a delightful smorgasbord of pleasures and treats. This is because, like most young men, you are controlled by your gonads.

Becoming the husband or father of one gives you a larger perspective on the consequences of unbridled sexuality and other
forms of self-indulgence. This is why marriage fundamentally
reorients your thinking. Those who pioneered the hedonism of
recent years and allowed it to continue far too late in life are
discovering this now.

A very basic and concrete reason demonstrates why marriage
is more than a piece of paper and why sex must be confined
as much as possible to marriage. Moreover, it is a reason that
concerns you directly as a man and one that you have a strong
self-interest in enforcing. For the brutal fact, counterintuitive as
it may seem, is that sex outside marriage hurts no one so much
as it hurts you. This is because the most important role of marriage is to create fatherhood. Marriage exists so that children
can have fathers.

Marriage was the traditional moral and legal means for a
man to become more than a sperm donor and instead acquire
the authority of a parent and father. Feminists understand this
when they renounce marriage as an institution of "patriarchy"
and promote single motherhood and divorce as positive goods
for their own sake. Instead of recognizing this truth, conservative
sentimentalists labor the cliché that marriage exists to civilize
men.[78] If so, that is part of a larger function: to protect the bond
between fathers and their children and, with it, the intact family.
This point, potentially the strongest in their case, is overlooked
by traditionalists who argue that marriage undergirds civilization.
For it is the father's presence that creates both the intact family
and the civil institution itself. The philosopher Thomas Hobbes

---

[78] E.g., Leon R. Kass, "The End of Courtship," *Public Interest* 126
(Winter 1997): 39–63.

attributed to married fatherhood a central role in the process of moving from primitive chaos to civilization. In nature, Hobbes argued, "the dominion is in the mother":

> For in the condition of mere nature, *where there are no matrimonial laws*, it cannot be known who is the father, unless it be declared by the mother: and therefore the right of dominion over the child dependeth on her will, and is consequently hers.

Only in civilization, where "matrimonial laws" do operate, is ultimate authority over children assumed by the father. Marriage creates both fatherhood and civilization. (Now do you see why philosophy can be useful?)

In fact, for all the ink spilled over delineating the proper role of the state in marriage, it is probably fair to say that the only essential role of the government in marriage is to guarantee the rights and authority of the parents, and especially the father.

Our legal system long insisted that marriage, not sperm, designates the father. The legal standard stipulated that a child born within wedlock is presumed to be that of the husband, because it enabled a marriage to survive the wife's adultery. (Earlier ages had a more balanced assessment of the female and male tendencies toward promiscuity.) The cuckolded husband was given the option of raising the interloper's child as his own in order to allow the marriage to remain intact and the child to have a father.

It is true that today marriage no longer affords any of these legal protections to fathers for which it originally existed. So you might think that marriage is indeed a sham. Why bother getting married?

Mounting evidence indicates that as men discover the terms of marriage and divorce today, they are engaging in an impromptu marriage "strike": refusing to marry or start families, knowing they can be criminalized if their wife walks out and how attractive the divorce industry has made it for her to do so.[79] And again, MGTOW has systematized this trend into a conscious movement.

This is understandable, but it is not a viable or healthy path for either a gentleman or a civilization. As a temporary stratagem to awaken the world into realizing that there will be no men to marry and no more babies to replenish the population (which are already major concerns) unless we undertake serious reform in the laws on divorce and child custody, it is perhaps defensible. But pursued as a permanent life choice, it is a humiliating defeat. Aside from forgoing the benefits described above, as a gentleman you are abdicating your responsibility to lead and conceding defeat before you have even engaged the enemy. Considering our theme of ruling, you are depriving yourself of the most fundamental domain that any man can rule: his home and family. The best training for ruling the world is by starting with those you love. Otherwise, why will you care for anyone else you might have occasion to rule? Would we not all rather have men ruling over us who received their training this way than those driven by personal ambition and craving for power?

This is precisely why feminism is so authoritarian. For feminists, wielding political power conflicts with family life and is an alternative to it, not an extension of it. It is driven by pure thirst for individual power.

This will marginalize you from not only ruling but effectively participating in society and invite morbid hedonism and self-pity.

---

[79] See Helen Smith, *Men on Strike: Why Men Are Boycotting Marriage, Fatherhood, and the American Dream—and Why It Matters* (New York: Encounter, 2014).

While you may have other, valid reasons for a life of celibacy, if you resort to it from fear, you will have largely disqualified yourself from being a gentleman.

I am assuming that you still want meaningful female companionship and possibly children. You certainly do not want to do this with a woman who does not value marriage. Because, without it, there is no hope of ever restoring the integrity of our families and our civilization itself. Marriage is still the only thing that gives you the authority of a father. Without this lifelong commitment, you are simply a sperm donor whom the mother and the courts can and mostly likely will discard at their whim. With it, you have the moral authority to show that you have played by the rules and that it is the lawyers, judges, clergy, journalists, and others who are not doing their jobs who must bear the burden of shame. At least you can hold your head high, whereas they must hide under the table, but often that is what it means to be a gentleman.

In short, it is in your interest and it is your responsibility to defend the integrity of marriage. You may even be required to defend it against the moralists who think that *they* are already the defenders of marriage. You disdain this responsibility at your peril, and you should defend it in both your personal life and your role as a civic leader. The destruction of marriage hurts no one so much as it hurts you and your children, but it is detrimental to all of society. Anything that weakens it — acts of fornication or adultery, cohabitation, illegitimacy, easy divorce, same-sex marriage — harms it and harms you. This includes your own acts of fornication or adultery and your own decision to cohabit with a woman. It also includes those of your friends. And you should offer advice to this effect to your family members and friends. Distasteful as our society has made this task, it is a reliable measure of true love, friendship, and courage.

Every major religion also insists on the sanctity of marriage (at least verbally), and it does so for a reason. This is one reason you should insist on getting married in a church. You want behind you the moral authority of an institution that upholds marriage as a permanent union. A civil ceremony alone implies that you accept the state's rules, which you are subject to anyway, but there is no need to give it a monopoly.

No society permits sexual chaos. Nowadays it is the feminists who are imposing their own regulations in the form of "sexual harassment" accusations. For, contrary to the propaganda, they do not favor sexual freedom any more than did the religious authorities. So you have a stark choice: either assume your natural role as voluntary enforcer of the rules—those that are tried and true—over yourself and those you love, or submit yourself and your family to the rule of the feminists and police.

Children

What was said about marriage also holds true of having children. For most of us, having children is part of what it means to be a complete human being. You have an instinct to reproduce that cannot be ignored. More to the point, it is integral to the ideal of a gentleman, which even in the common acceptation of the word offers every man the possibility of a quasi-aristocratic pedigree. Every man is proud of his name and wants to pass it on. A gentleman honors what he owes to both past and future generations. He acknowledges what he has inherited from those before and his stake in the well-being of others after he is gone.

Having children also helps gives you a sense of responsibility, not only toward your own children but also toward the rest of the world. This is not because you adopt the role of *paterfamilias* and treat the world as if they are your children. Quite the opposite, there is nothing like being a parent to teach you the difference between what really belongs among your own essential responsibilities and what is none of your business. This is because you quickly develop an acute sense of what is none of the rest of the world's business. And with your own children you are essential and cannot be replaced.

Yet, as with marriage, having children is another area where young gentlemen have a challenge these days. Practically speaking, the decision to have children is today a matter of choice, as children are no longer an economic necessity or even asset for most people. On the contrary, for most people they are a major economic burden, which is why most people now have few. Training up those who will contribute to the household economy, and gradually assume responsibility for it, was a major incentive for a gentleman to pass on his values as well as his wealth.

Not only that, but despite all the pieties nowadays about everything being "for the children," the harsh reality is that children's lack of economic value has resulted in a serious deterioration of their status and lives. Now they are ruthlessly exploited as pawns in games of power played by grown-ups, all claiming to uphold "the best interest of the child," even children whom they do not know or love. Children today have almost everything they want and little of what they need.

But even more seriously, for a man today there is one critical rule to remember: once you have a child, you lose all your rights. And I mean all of them. The moment a child is born, he is the property of the state, and he resides with you and you raise him at the pleasure of government officials. (This is true of your wife as well.) The moment a man has a child—and without committing any legal transgression—he can be deprived of not only that child and any future children, but also his home, his savings and assets, and his future earnings; every corner of his private life can be investigated; his movements can be restricted and controlled; he can be interrogated behind closed doors; his public utterances, publications, and Internet writings can be monitored and censored, and he can be jailed indefinitely without charge and without trial. This is the reality, and short of legal reform, there is nothing you can do to change it. Almost daily, I am asked how a man can protect himself legally in advance against the loss of his children and everything else by family court. The answer, quite simply, is that he cannot. Pre-nuptial agreements? No provision involving children is enforceable in law. Arbitration agreements? Likewise unenforceable. The moment you produce a child, you are at the mercy of the mother and any lawyers or government officials she chooses to enlist. In fact, she can find herself at their mercy as well. And people wonder why the birth rate is in free fall.

So why should you persist in wanting children? In addition to the reasons given above, a gentleman does not cower or retreat permanently in the face of the enemy. If economics and lawyers are conspiring to deprive you and other men of families and posterity (plus other little matters, such as constitutional rights), the solution is not submission but defiance—defiance alongside other gentlemen against those who want to snuff out not only the gentlemanly ideal but also future gentlemen (and ladies). Your children themselves provide your major motivation for this. Allowing fear to deprive you of this most basic of human and civilizational needs puts you in a posture of habitual submission. Whatever trappings of a gentleman you acquire, much of the substance will lost.

In case it matters, you are also very likely acquiescing in the downward spiral of your own society, and not simply because of an absence of babies. Remember what we said about marriage: fatherhood and civilization are created together. Lose one, and you lose both.

Once you have children, the same principles that are valid for you are valid for them, and it is the role of a father to pass down his knowledge, wisdom, and wealth to both his sons and daughters. As for the principles of child-rearing, that must await a separate book devoted entirely to this topic alone.

Finances

An ability to manage the family estate responsibly is another mark of a true gentleman. You may not have bands of retainers and vassals or fields full of tenants and serfs; perhaps you do not even have a household of servants. But we each have been allotted something of which we are the stewards, and this is the attitude you should adopt, if you have not already, as you embark on married and family life. The basics of money management, saving, and investment can be acquired from a number of sources, including banks, investment firms, financial advisers, and, of course, with caution, the Internet. Given the ubiquity of lawsuits today — in America and increasingly other countries, it is a truism among lawyers, who readily act upon it, that "anybody can sue anybody for anything" — it is very likely you will at least be threatened with one. It is a good idea to learn about trusts and create one.

Normally, I would not have expected that such a section as this would be necessary. But I was aghast to find what other modern etiquette and advice books are now promoting. One suggests that, if couples cannot agree on financial arrangements, they should simply keep separate accounts. The author's sole authority for this sage counsel is none other than the professional association of the divorce lawyers. This is hardly accidental. Such advice not only facilitates their work but encourages more of it.

The fact that an etiquette manual can counsel married couples to treat their household affairs like a college fraternity house confirms my own view that only one arrangement is defensible. When it comes to marital and family finances, they are to be merged and in common. Moreover, you are in charge of them. This must be understood before the marriage. If she objects to this arrangement, this is a big red flag.

Unless you are incapacitated, the only reason for the woman to manage the family finances is to put herself in an advantageous position to divorce you. There is no clearer indication of a woman's proclivity for divorce than her desire to keep separate financial accounts, and nothing makes it easier for her to divorce, though you should be under no illusion that this will protect your assets and prevent you from having to pay her large sums of money or from plunder by the lawyers. Most certainly it will not.

If you yourself manage the finances for such a purpose, first, you have seriously misunderstood what marriage is for, and you are not ready for it. More dangerously, you are on a fool's errand and have a serious misunderstanding of how divorce works. A judge can and will simply take whatever he wants and give it to her, or to the lawyers, or to his other cronies, or keep it for himself.

The family is the most basic economic unit of society; in fact, it is the only such unit that produces general prosperity. If it is not a unified economic unit, then it is not a family. It is the one institution that can — indeed, must — work according to the principle of "from each according to his ability, to each according to his needs" — which is another reason it must be indissoluble, to prevent the one with ability, at any given moment, to desert the ones with needs. Moreover, a marriage is the joining of not simply two people but of two families. If she prefers to continue living like two university students, then she is not ready for marriage, and you should drop the idea.

Some traditional authorities do advise reserving a small sum attached exclusively to the wife, as a protection against business risks, lawsuits, or bad tendencies of the husband such as drinking and gambling. If such possibilities exist — and again, the lawsuits most certainly do, even if you cannot imagine having injured anyone — this may be advisable and not necessarily inconsistent with the principle stated above, so long as you are clear about the purpose.

Needless to say, you are not a dictator with the family finances. But you cannot be, because as long as your marriage is indissoluble, which it must be, your decisions will permanently affect you together with everyone else. You must manage them for the long-term solvency and welfare of the entire family, including members who are not yet born. Managing the finances does not mean using them for yourself, and if you manage them wisely, there can be no conflict between what is in your interest or her interest and the long-term interest of the entire "firm."

You should consult your wife before major financial decisions or purchases — if she wishes to be consulted. Many women do not and prefer that the man handle all the financial matters. Remember, you are the one who will be held responsible when matters go wrong, so it is important that you both accept this responsibility and maintain the control. Consult your wife before substantial expenditures that are only for yourself. On the other hand, you must allow her to make substantial purchases for herself, and you will encounter problems if you are parsimonious about that. Think of her spending on clothes, makeup, hairdressers, naughty underwear, and so forth as gifts for you as well as items for herself. You should provide the jewelry, as gifts to mark special occasions, which she will also appreciate. Again, do not be stingy. Jewelry is not the most efficient financial investment, but neither is it irresponsible. Likewise for matters such as the kitchen, bathroom, furniture, and other household affairs, allow her what she needs. If you think she is spending to make herself appealing to other men, you have a problem and must step in.

Divorce

Yours

I receive letters, calls, and e-mail messages almost daily, and they always begin with words like this: "You won't believe what happened to me." But I do believe it, because not only have I witnessed many such cases; I have written entire books explaining why it happens.

Here I will distill all that down to practical information, though I must confess that there is not a lot to offer. Some may sound harsh and counterintuitive, and you may have to unlearn some conventional wisdom. For the standard "how-to" manuals on divorce written by lawyers and other divorce practitioners are full of self-serving platitudes that could hurt you badly.

First, it should be understood that, on your part, divorce is not really an option. You have given your word as a gentleman, and you are required to keep it. Marriage is a lifelong commitment, and it works only if that is understood. And again, if nothing else, this is in your self-interest and everyone else's, because if marriage establishes fatherhood, divorce destroys it. Beyond simply acknowledging legally your wife's desertion or adultery, you have no business undertaking legal action against your family. Marshaling the public justice system and other government machinery against family members, especially one to whom you have sworn lifelong love and honor, for private differences forfeits the moral high ground, is unmanly, and surrenders to the state your authority over your family. You will deserve whatever opprobrium people heap on you. Sorry, but you cannot have it both ways, complaining about the depredations of the divorce system and then trying to take advantage of it yourself.

That said, the harsh reality is that divorce can be, and usually is, inflicted unilaterally and involuntarily on men, without their having given any legal grounds ("no-fault"). From here on, we will assume that this is the case for you.

You must also understand that if your wife files for divorce, there is a good chance that you are the one who will be blamed. You will be blamed by the courts, social workers, psychologists, and counselors, because it is in their financial interest to blame you. But you may also be blamed by family members, including your own children. This is even if you are legally blameless and you object strenuously to the whole divorce in the first place. Your wife can desert the home, carry on a half dozen affairs, abuse the children, and file for divorce with no grounds, and it is likely that you will be blamed.

This will strike you as bizarre and irrational. You may react like many men: "anti-father bias" proceeding from "stereotypes" needs to change though a campaign for "gender equality," and so forth. This jargon will not help you. It will only frustrate you and encourage you to bitterness and self-pity and inspire contempt in others. What you are witnessing is the unchangeable order of the universe. It is a universal principle that the man is always held responsible for his family. The divorce courts have simply manipulated this truth for their own purposes. This is why you must always hold the ultimate decision-making authority.

Relinquish it, and you will then serve no practical purpose and become disposable.

You must further understand that the divorce courts are not "unfair" or "inefficient," and the judges are not "biased" or "stupid" or in need of "education." They are crooked. They know precisely what they are doing, and they do it with ruthless efficiency. They may mouth feminist clichés one moment, and then turn around and profess pieties about traditional motherhood the next, but these simply rationalize what really drives them, which is money and power. The courts are run by venal judges, lawyers, and civil servants who are all united in one object: to take control over your children and use them as leverage to loot and criminalize you. The first principle and first action of divorce court is to separate children from their fathers and keep them apart as much as possible.

This is not cynicism; it is simply the way the system operates. Nothing is served by directing anger against the judge or lawyers. They, too, are effectively prisoners of the system (albeit well paid ones). Any judge or lawyer who tries to administer honest justice will himself be punished.

This is why they cannot be persuaded by logic or morality. If the courts do not seize control over your children, they have no reason to exist, and the huge entourage of functionaries they employ would have no work and no earnings. Never waste your time, money, or sanity trying to obtain justice from the courts. You will not.

The divorce manuals written by lawyers, therapists, and other divorce operators are full of pious sanctimonies professing concern for your children. But no divorce practitioner ever lost a minute's sleep over your children. "I don't love your children," one judge confesses. "It is a legal fiction that the law's best interest is your children."[80] None has ever done or will do anything for your child that they are not well paid to do. In the eyes of lawyers and functionaries, your children are walking bundles of cash. Whoever gets control of them gets the cash, from either the taxpayers or your bank account. Sanctimonious professions of concern about your children and other people's children are their most potent weapon. Great courage on your part is needed to stand against it, because those posturing as children's defenders can make themselves credible only by casting you as the greatest threat to the welfare and safety of your own children.

None of this is to say you can "win" by listening to me. You cannot. There is no way to "win" in divorce court. The only way to avoid losing your children is not to have them in the first place.

So what do you do when you come home one day, the children are gone, and you find a note from your wife and a summons from the court? Frankly, there is not much you can do. You must prepare yourself psychologically to lose your home, your savings, and, most importantly, your children. You could soon face child support payments so high that you will soon become homeless, and if you cannot pay, you will be sent to jail indefinitely with no trial. All this can happen within days or even hours.

First, you must set aside all pious sanctimony about doing the right thing in the courts. You will not be rewarded for it, and it could cost you dearly. Doing the right thing means rescuing your children from the clutches of the divorce operatives, who will certainly exploit and destroy them, and then staying out of jail yourself.

The moment you walk into a courtroom, the first thing the judge will do is legally remove your children from your care and

---

[80] Stephen Barr, "Refereeing the Ugliest Game in Town," *New Jersey Monthly* (May 1998): 52–55, 71–74.

control. The order will be called "temporary," but from this moment on and for the rest of their childhood, you may have no contact with your children without court authorization, and anything you do without permission subjects you to incarceration without trial. No burden of proof requires the court to justify this action. The burden of proof—and the enormous expense it entails—is now on you to get them back.

The typical response of men who harbor the illusion that they are in charge and capable of manly action is that "I am going to hire the most aggressive kick-ass lawyer I can who will go in there and do what it takes." Fine, but you must realize that your lawyer is not really on your side. He is in collusion with the other lawyer and the judge, and their aim is to maximize the litigation and drive up the fees as much as possible for all concerned. You can gauge his honesty by how much he acknowledges this reality. If he promises you the moon (or simple justice), he is on the take. If he is honest about how powerless he is to help you, then he is probably stuck in a game he does not like. For if he were truly honest, he would soon be disbarred.

One measure can help maintain some semblance of justice and accountability: *never* go to court without hiring your own court reporter to record everything. It is expensive, but it can save you money and trouble in the long run. Try to hire one from a different jurisdiction, because reporters are pressured by judges and lawyers to falsify transcripts. Yes, the courts are that corrupt.

In the end, your only constructive course of action is to object publicly—and loudly. If you have any public profile—as a lawyer, journalist, writer, clergyman, professor, businessman—you can use it to publicize the injustice. Simply as a citizen and householder with a family to defend, you can take the moral high ground and proclaim the truth: write letters to the editor;

get editorials published in the newspaper; approach television stations; make a big noise. Like all corrupt officials, judges hate exposure. This action can backfire on you, and the judge can punish you for it, though that, in turn, can look bad for him. If you are at all successful, it can even provide you some protection by informing the judge that what he does will be exposed to public view. You must gauge the likelihood for success of this for yourself. This is consistent with your duty as a leader.

OTHERS'

This is a touchy subject and challenges your fortitude as a man. I shall certainly receive scorn for prescribing what used to be the universally accepted norm. What do you do when family and friends betray other family and friends? When people you love do things that are wrong, it is your obligation to tell them. You are not showing true love or being a true friend if you fail in this.

While many areas of life are appropriate for applying this principle, divorce is especially imperative today, though it is also the least likely to see it applied. Strikingly, all the modern etiquette books that address it merely encourage you to renege on your duty. They urge you, somehow, to keep out of it while maintaining tact and good relations. In short, they advise you (as if any of us need such advising) to be a spineless wimp. Here is how one respected etiquette book dodges the issue:

> Unless a couple is separating under extremely good terms, I recommend that lawyers handle the proceedings whenever possible.[81]

---

[81] Charlotte Ford, *21st Century Etiquette: A Guide to Manners for the Modern Age* (New York: Barnes & Noble, 2011), 190.

Of course she does, because she wants to avoid not only awk-wardness but especially the enormous moral issues. She wants to avoid dealing with your emasculation. The situation is unavoid-ably awkward because someone is misbehaving egregiously, and everyone else is pretending not to notice. At least one loved one or friend needs your help, and if you stay out of it, you are not a friend but a coward.

Divorce today is highly unlikely to be completely amicable. Far more likely is that one spouse is unilaterally enlisting lawyers and courts to attack, loot, or revenge herself or himself upon the other. As an interested party, it is your job to ascertain what happened and who is at fault and to intervene on behalf of the wronged spouse.

I do not want to hear about how it is "none of my business." If you are a family member, it is a family affair. If you are a friend, it is a duty of friendship. Otherwise, families and friendships mean nothing to you, and you are a shallow person. And if you do not intervene, the lawyers and judges will, with the police and jailers close behind.

In the case of an affair or a divorce, you are well within the bounds of propriety and morality—indeed, you are obligated—to snub the misbehaving spouse along with any interloper.

This principle—greatly watered down—is suggested by one of today's popular manners writers, Judith Martin, better known as Miss Manners.[82] I regard Miss Manners as one of the better modern etiquette guides, so I will pick on her to show where she abandons her own sound principles.

---

[82] The following quotations are taken from Judith Martin, *Miss Manners' Guide to Excruciatingly Correct Behavior* (New York: Norton, 2005), 190, 663, 265–267.

"Whatever else divorce may be for children, it is a severe etiquette problem," she writes. Distinguishing an "etiquette problem" from a "moral problem," she claims to concern herself only with the first. Sorry, but it is not so simple. If etiquette is to mean anything other than the finishing school that cynics see in it, it inevitably concerns morals. Traditionally, moral codes were enforced through codes of "manners," in the old sense, and if we do not want them further enforced through the gendarmerie, we must understand how this worked and recover what we can of it.

When one is faced with serious misbehavior involving marital infidelity, Miss Manners offers an uncharacteristically awkward response, reflecting the inherent awkwardness the matter invariably presents: "At the [twentieth] century's beginning, everyone touched by such a situation would have become a permanent social outcast." Today's weaker standards, however, allow evasion by both the family and the advice book. "The aggrieved party would be at fault for not getting over it (as your family argues)," she tells a reader, "and her supporters for being judgmental." Miss Manners' own advice is as pusillanimous as the family's response, suggesting that they avoid situations where the woman must interact with the sister and former husband who ran off together (which is, no doubt, what they are already doing). Whatever else this is, it is not a manly response.

The jilted spouse herself is permitted stronger measures, when interacting with the new girlfriend, but she must manage this on her own:

Cool behavior consists of doing everything socially required in a correct but abbreviated fashion. You greet the person with a short smile indicated by the turning up of the corners of the mouth but no accompanying sign of pleasure in the eyes. You answer any questions in few, neutral words ("Thank you, I'm fine."), avoid asking any of your own ("I trust you are well" can substitute for "How are you?") and seize the first opportunity to say "Excuse me" and turn away.

Should this fail—should your former friend attempt, for example, to hug you—Miss Manners gives you permission to turn it up to Frosty. At that setting, "Excuse me" immediately follows the greeting.

If this is the proper response by the jilted spouse herself or himself, why not for her family and all who claim her friendship, both to show support and uphold what were at one time the community's standards?

Later, she writes that "shunning scoundrels is one of society's duties, sadly neglected by those who refuse to pass judgment," as she herself has just done. Apparently scoundrel status is reserved for an accused (but not convicted) child molester—that is, an alleged criminal who has not had his day in court. He alone merits the harshest penalty: excommunication, or what she calls "a modified form of shunning":

> Rather than pointedly withdrawing your hand if he tries to shake it, you occupy it by patting your hair; rather than turn your back if he approaches you, you say "Excuse me" and turn to go elsewhere; rather than greeting any friendly overtures with silence, you respond only with a nod. Above all, you refuse to smile or to discuss "what's wrong." The punishments of etiquette may sound weak, but Miss Manners assures you that to be treated coldly with no opportunity to explain is frightening.

Indeed it is, and using them more would reduce our dependency on police, courts, and lawyers.

Miss Manners' own responses here reflect a deterioration of standards. One might have thought that an accused criminal should be confronted with the accusation against him and reported to the police. If convicted, he should then be jailed. Or, if it turns out that he is innocent (a real possibility nowadays), he should be left in peace.

The sanctions she prescribes for him are, in fact, precisely the ones appropriate for matters such as adultery and involuntary, unilateral divorce itself. Miss Manners has provided a perfect description of precisely the response that was traditionally and universally considered appropriate for any friends, family members, or acquaintances who use the instruments of your government to unjustly deprive another of his or her home, children, property, or freedom.

But it is a certainty that Miss Manners' books would no longer be published were she to demonstrate such backbone. You must show that you have a stronger spine.

The new rules governing divorce encapsulate a larger lesson that you must absorb about being a man nowadays. The rules may seem bizarre, irrational, unbelievable, insane—these are the words men use most often when they discover what they are up against. But they are none of these things. The new rules were put in place by clever people—radical ideologues, assisted by lawyers and government bureaucrats—who knew exactly what they were doing. They are the culmination of trends that have been at work for many decades if not centuries, and they are only the beginning. The divorce laws are simply the logical outcome of today's larger rules for relations between the sexes, which likewise have lulled men into a feminine passivity where they are defenseless against being cast as society's villains. The divorce laws, therefore, provide an appropriate starting point for navigating and surviving under those new rules.

CONCLUSION

As society closes in on you and your manhood, you have a choice: you can try to continue living the unmanly passivity that got us all into this in the first place. You can keep your head down, hide under the table, and hope they find someone else to lock in the pillory. You can spend your patrimony hiring therapists to make yourself feel better and lawyers to fight your battles for you. And then, when, despite all this, you inevitably lose — because you can never really win — you can complain that it is all so "unfair." Here you will be accused of being a crybaby, and indeed, you will sink deeper into the human default status, which is female. You can even complain that you are the victim of "sexism," that you have suffered "discrimination" and been made a "second-class citizen," and that all you are asking for is "gender equality." Thus, you will become the mirror image of the very people who are doing their best to emasculate you. But they will not be impressed, and neither will anyone else. Instead, they will smile with satisfaction as they listen to you parrot the very grievances, expressed in their own jargon, that they have leveled against you and all men as "oppressors." Now they have you, mind and soul as well as body. You are now fighting on your enemies' terms, and by doing so, you have already conceded the battle. But no one will listen or care. They will just chuckle to themselves as they cynically tell you to "act like a man."

And what will you say then? It is far better to resolve simply to be a man from the start.

Aping their own "oppressors" has been the general response of many men throughout the gender wars, which is why the courts and welfare agencies continue to degenerate into an extortion racket, men continue to be locked up to the tune of two million in the United States alone, and the noose of the state gendarmerie and penal machinery tightens around all of us. So many mechanisms now exist for turning men into criminals and putting them in jail and prison that there is also hardly a male in the Western world who has not been threatened with at least one.

But while it is appropriate to invoke your rights in the proper context, remember that the Rights of Man alone can never protect you from the Reign of Terror, because the same people who first issue the Rights are the ones who later instigate the Terror. Before they terrorize, they first corner the market on the rights—and the corresponding grievances, disarming their victims of any right to complain. "No freedom for the enemies of freedom!" as they used to say in the French Revolution. Both sexes are equal, George Orwell might have said. But now one is more equal than the other.

Your other option is to stand up right now and begin indeed to act like a man. You must claim the moral high ground and start to stand up for yourself, for other men, and for women, children, and everyone else. You start to be a leader. You start to be a man.

You may object that you have already proven your manhood. Perhaps you have served your country in uniform or in dangerous occupations like law enforcement or construction or aviation. Sorry, but this is no longer enough. You must be not only an officer but also a gentleman. Your physical courage must be matched with moral courage.

If you choose this option, you will need to adopt a new way of thinking. You will need to abandon the default status, which is passive and quasi-female, and adopt a proactive mind. You will start to think differently about yourself and about the world. It will be difficult and perhaps frightening at first to abandon your comfort zone. You must renounce the intoxication that comes from moral superiority and accept the risks and sacrifices inherent to manhood. But as you do so, you will begin to experience a feeling of great freedom and release.

You may object that you do not endorse "political correctness" and even ridicule it. This is unlikely. For we are all acculturated to it, however little we may realize it. Realizing how far our own minds are enslaved to today's culture is the first step in emancipating ourselves from it.

Ridding your mind of the remnants of ideology is not easy, but this book should have helped. I can say this because I have spent nearly forty years of professional study on political topics in general and almost twenty-five years on these topics in particular. Much of that task has been to rid my own mind of the politically correct habits in which I was raised. Daily discoveries remind me that I have not fully completed this task myself and perhaps never will. Trite clichés such as "sexism," "discrimination," and "gender bias" are only the most obvious. These terms are a sure sign that someone is pulling the wool over your eyes. But remember that *anything* you read in the newspaper or hear in the media concerning men and women is distorted to serve someone's agenda.

This book has described principles that, until a few years ago, would have been considered common sense and accepted

without question or debate. Some were shared by almost all civilized societies through thousands of years of human history, but
all were ingredients in Western society, which is the most successful civilization in history. Today these principles have been
relabeled by a small elite with an agenda, using new, pejorative
terms that no one really understands because they have no fixed
meaning and can be expanded to mean anything that a man like
you might say or do: "sexism," "misogyny," "homophobia," "hate
speech." These labels mean only that you should feel ashamed
of disagreeing with the moral prig who is mouthing them. But
nowadays they may also be grounds for legal action or even criminal prosecution. This vocabulary is the language of ideology, not
the product of educated thought or accumulated wisdom. It is
the ideology into which we have all been acculturated and pressured in this generation, and these prepackaged buzzwords are
the complacent party jargon that substitute for not only thought
but also common decency. If you find these clichés comforting,
then your mind is still in thrall to ideology, and you are not free.
Moral understanding is critical to being a gentleman. Moralistic
posturing simply makes you a prig.

 This, too, is an issue of manhood, to be "self-reliant," as Emerson put it. Men do not hire other men (let alone women) to
fight their battles for them. As journalist Melinda Blau observes,
this is chiefly a feminine trait. "Women are particularly vulner-
able to lawyers," she writes, "only to discover that they are not
the knights in shining armor we had hoped for—far from it."[83]
Obviously, you must occasionally employ lawyers and other hired
hands, much as you might hire other men to work on your house.

---

[83] Melinda Blau, *Families Apart: Ten Keys to Successful Co-Parenting*
 (New York: Putnam, 1993), 89.

Conclusion

But, in both cases, you must keep an eye on what they are doing. Harbor no illusions about what you are doing and why this has become so unavoidable. Lawyers occupy a gray zone between private citizens and government functionaries, and while they are ostensibly there to protect the citizens, their own self-interest lies in appeasing their masters in the state. Lawyers are our professional surrogate citizens. They are people we hire to perform the duties of citizenship for us. When we farm out our citizenship by hiring judicial mercenaries to fight our civic battles, then they become our masters, much the way mercenary soldiers will readily turn on those who hire them. This is why we can no longer protect ourselves from the state without hiring its operatives. True men would dispense with lawyers altogether and defend themselves. But we are not true men any longer. Any of us.

But this has not been entirely a book about how to survive against the government and its hangers-on. It is also about avoiding them in the first place. And, in the long run, it is about disarming them for all men and all women. In other words, it is about living a normal life.

So do not worry, I am not insisting that you drop everything and devote your life to some righteous political campaign. Being a gentleman does not mean becoming a zealous political activist; quite the opposite. Today, it is largely a matter of protecting yourself and those around you from all the other zealous political activists. It is about standing your ground as a man, a father, a husband, and a citizen. It does not mean devoting your life to righteous crusades undertaken in the name of stirring abstract and universal "causes." It means defending yourself and those closest to you and defending the principles of freedom, mostly nowadays from people whose righteous crusades have reached a point of such absurdity that they cast ordinary men like you as criminals.

A GENTLEMAN'S GUIDE

We as a civilization have a decision to make. That question, quite simply, is whether we are willing to recognize and value any distinctive masculinity at all and content to relegate men to the status of second-rate women (thereby consigning women to the role of second-rate men). If not, it will require a much greater commitment of effort than we have been willing to exert so far. This starts with you.

The relations between men and women have long been governed by elaborate rules of the kind described in this book, and the purpose was to protect everyone from, among other things, the destructive power of uncontrolled sexual urges. Among the institutions these rules protected was the role of men in the family and throughout society. These rules were grounded in traditional morality and religion, but today they have been largely replaced by other rules grounded in political ideology and government power. In permitting and promoting this change, let us not pretend that all the gender faults were or are on one side. Men had a role at least as great as that of women in breaking down these rules, and now they are paying the consequences. If you want to restore your status as a man, you must accept your role in reestablishing the rules. There are no shortcuts. You cannot regain the status of a man while enjoying the pleasures of an adolescent.

So what is the secret to being a gentleman? What is the most basic principle required to start on this path? As we have seen, this question has been debated at length over the centuries, but perhaps it is only now, as we are in danger of losing it (like Hegel's owl of Minerva, which flies in the evening), that we are really in a position to realize the essence of what we are losing.

Conclusion

If there is one principle that succinctly epitomizes a gentleman and will start you on the path to becoming one, though one
that may be especially difficult to apply in today's circumstances,
it is this: *Stop rebelling*. Stop adopting the stance that the world
is unfair and that it is your job to take every opportunity to tell
the world why it is so unfair. Yes, you and other men may indeed
be the most graphic illustrations and the greatest targets of that
unfairness today, and you are indeed likely to be genuine victims,
in contrast to all the other pseudo- and self-proclaimed victims,
but this makes the point even stronger. Your oppressors have
cornered the market on not only victimhood but also on rebellion
(including terms like "oppressors"), so it is no longer available
to you. But that is good. The time for rebellion was adolescence,
and the person to rebel against was your father, whose job it was
to teach you how to rebel responsibly and constructively. If, as
is likely nowadays, you and your father were deprived of this
experience together, if you never had a father in the first place
or if yours was weak and never taught you this, then pondering
this principle may at least help you come to terms with that void
in your upbringing. We all have some, after all. But that does not
justify perpetuating your lost adolescent rebellion throughout
the rest of what should be your mature life. If you are a male
over the age of eighteen, then you are part of the ruling class,
even if it does not feel like it when you are being hauled away in
handcuffs. Ironic as it may seem sometimes, you are still, and you
are always and inevitably, the one being rebelled *against*, even
if you no longer have any power. Responding to the insurgents
by launching your own counterinsurgency will just inflame the
chaos, surrender the moral high ground, and not help you or
anyone else. The moment you put away your rebellion is the
moment you will assume your rightful place and begin to rule.

A GENTLEMAN'S GUIDE

Like it or not, the ball is now in your court. (Actually, the ball is always in your court.) So stop complaining and start acting your age and your role. You have a stake in the world, and you are responsible for what you pass on to the next generation. Otherwise, when future generations look back on our times and assess what went wrong, they will (like everyone else) blame you for the mess made by others, even when you had no part in creating it. No one ever said that ruling the world would be easy.

ABOUT THE AUTHOR

The author is a university lecturer of more than thirty years' experience. He is also a certified gentleman, not because he has a coat of arms (though he does) but because he is married to a genuine lady. Currently they reside in a republic, but he is trying his best to change that.

Sophia Institute

Sophia Institute is a nonprofit institution that seeks to nurture the spiritual, moral, and cultural life of souls and to spread the gospel of Christ in conformity with the authentic teachings of the Roman Catholic Church.

Sophia Institute Press fulfills this mission by offering translations, reprints, and new publications that afford readers a rich source of the enduring wisdom of mankind.

Sophia Institute also operates the popular online resource CatholicExchange.com. *Catholic Exchange* provides world news from a Catholic perspective as well as daily devotionals and articles that will help readers to grow in holiness and live a life consistent with the teachings of the Church.

In 2013, Sophia Institute launched Sophia Institute for Teachers to renew and rebuild Catholic culture through service to Catholic education. With the goal of nurturing the spiritual, moral, and cultural life of souls, and an abiding respect for the role and work of teachers, we strive to provide materials and programs that are at once enlightening to the mind and ennobling to the heart; faithful and complete, as well as useful and practical.

Sophia Institute gratefully recognizes the Solidarity Association for preserving and encouraging the growth of our apostolate over the course of many years. Without their generous and timely support, this book would not be in your hands.

www.SophiaInstitute.com
www.CatholicExchange.com
www.SophiaInstituteforTeachers.org

Sophia Institute Press® is a registered trademark of Sophia Institute.
Sophia Institute is a tax-exempt institution as defined by the
Internal Revenue Code, Section 501(c)(3). Tax ID 22-2548708.

		DATE DUE		

St. Stephen the Martyr Catholic Church
13055 SE 192nd St,
Renton, WA 98058